L. RON HUBBARD

THE WRITER

The Shaping of Popular Fiction

CONTENTS

ISBN 1-57318-060-2

© 1997 L. Ron Hubbard Library. All Rights Reserved.

Dianetics, Scientology, LRH, Writers of The Future, the LRH Device, and the RON Signature are trademarks and service marks owned by Religious Technology Center and are used with its permission.

The Writers of The Future Logo is a trademark owned by L. Ron Hubbard Library.

Photographs appearing on pages 16, 17, 18–19, 20, 23, 46, 47, 48, 51 and 54 courtesy of American Stock Photography; page 66 courtesy of Goldberg/FPG; page 77 courtesy of New York City Public Library, page 76 (top left) courtesy Jay Kaye Kline.

An Introduction to
L. Ron Hubbard

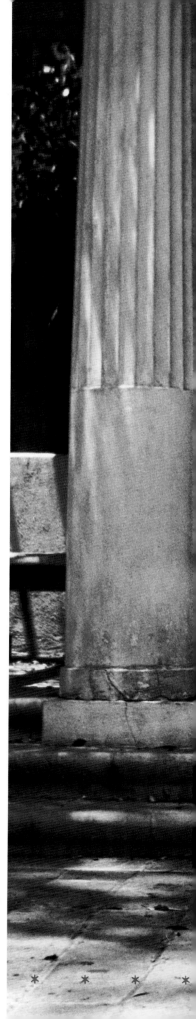

FOR ALL THE NAME L. RON HUBBARD REPRESENTS AS THE FOUNDER OF Dianetics and Scientology, let us never lose sight of the man as an author—specifically, among the world's most enduring and widely read authors of popular fiction, with international sales approaching forty million and a body of work spanning fifty years. Nor let us lose sight of his greater impact; he is legitimately credited with helping to reshape whole genres through the 1930s and 1940s, while his eleven consecutive *New York Times* bestsellers from the 1980s still mark an unequaled event in publishing history. Then, too, let us never lose sight of all he represented in the name of authorship as a profession—which is to say, all that is presented here as L. Ron Hubbard addresses the craft of writing.

Included are essays, articles and notes from the whole of those fifty years as a leading light of popular fiction. That we find L. Ron Hubbard devoted so much in explanation of creative writing is typical of a man who authored the singularly most influential philosophic statement on artistic creativity, *Art*. It is likewise typical of a man who founded the singularly most prestigious program for the discovery of young talent within speculative fiction, the internationally acclaimed Writers of The Future Contest. Then again, it is typical of an American Fiction Guild president who worked so doggedly on behalf of emerging talent through the Great Depression, the voice of new authors from the Pacific Northwest and a regular voice of encouragement to colleagues in need. But quite apart from all other efforts to instruct and inspire, we are about to discover how L. Ron Hubbard himself approached the blank page—how he conceived of ideas, executed those ideas and otherwise attended to what he first and foremost described as "this business of writing."

* * * * * * * * * * * * * * * *

It would prove a lifelong occupation. His earliest published stories date from 1932, or his sophomore year at George Washington University where three LRH works appear among the pages of the student quarterly: two tragic tales drawn from travels across Asia, and the existential narrative of a sailor who has glimpsed his own death in a San Diego movie house. For whatever it's worth, the stories are miles better than the maudlin stuff from fellow undergraduates and, arguably, the finest work to emerge from the George Washington literary department. Beyond university, and following much in the way of raw adventure through the course of two Caribbean expeditions, he set himself to a fully professional literary pursuit—in particular, supplying short stories to that legendary vehicle of popular fiction, the rough stock periodicals otherwise known as the pulps.

The pulps—name alone still conjures images of high adventure in exotic realms: Tarzan and Doc Savage stalking crazed killers through beast-infested jungles, the Shadow and Phantom hunting equally nefarious creatures through a grim urban nether world. And if critics of the day generally dismissed it all as lowbrow escapism, the best of those pulps represented a lot more. For example, with the likes of Dashiell Hammett, Raymond Chandler and Tennessee Williams all setting forth from the pages of pulps, those pages finally gave as much to the modern American novel as a Hemingway or Fitzgerald. (Chandler probably described it best as that literature reflecting "a sharp, aggressive attitude towards life . . . spare, frugal, hard-boiled . . .") Then, too, with a full quarter of the American population regularly turning to those crudely cut pages, the pulps did far more than a

Henry James or a Stephen Crane to introduce a nation to the sheer joy of reading.

What L. Ron Hubbard wrought in that great pulp kingdom was ultimately just as significant and just as transcendent. "As perfect a piece of science fiction as has ever been written," declared Robert Heinlein of the apocalyptic *Final Blackout;* while elsewhere we find that LRH tale of a war without end repeatedly described as surpassing all science fiction offered as of 1940. Representing no less to the realm of modern fantasy is the perennially popular *Fear,* broadly acknowledged as a pillar of all modern horror and, as master of the genre Stephen King proclaimed, one of the few in the genre "which actually merits employment of the overworked adjective 'classic,' as in 'This is a classic tale of creeping, surreal menace and horror.' "

One could say more, particularly regarding the extraordinary critical and popular success of the later LRH. The internationally bestselling *Battlefield Earth: A Saga of the Year 3000,* for example, not only stands as the largest single volume of science fiction to date, but among the most honored. In addition to both the Academy of Science Fiction, Fantasy and Horror Films' Golden Scroll and Saturn Awards, the work has earned Italy's Tetradramma D'Oro Award (in recognition of the story's inherent message of peace) and a special Gutenberg Award as an exceptional contribution to the genre. Similarly honored was the ten-volume *Mission Earth* series, each topping international bestseller lists in what amounted to a publishing phenomenon and cumulatively earning both the Cosmos 2000 Award from French readers and Italy's Nova Science Fiction Award.

Then again, one could cite all L. Ron Hubbard represents as the model author in many a university—very much including the L. Ron Hubbard wing of Moscow University's Gorky Library—and all else he represents to modern fiction as a whole: ". . . one of the most prolific and influential writers of the twentieth century," to quote critic and educator Stephen V. Whaley. But it is finally not the purpose of this publication to merely celebrate the author, L. Ron Hubbard; our purpose is to learn from him.

Among the various essays to follow, LRH makes reference to a certain "professor of short story . . . [who] knew nothing about the practical end of things." We happen to know that professor as Douglas Bement of George Washington University—apparently well-meaning, but fairly obsessed with all the claptrap of academic criticism, including the intentional foreshadow, the timely *denouement*, the pervasive mood and carefully wrought allegory. As an undergraduate, Ron confesses to learning nothing; while as a later guest at the lectern, he tells of inciting a virtual revolt when defining a viable production rate in terms of a hundred thousand words a month. (So much for the carefully wrought allegory.) But in either case, and for all that is indeed carefully wrought in the LRH short story, he offers none of the Bement verbiage.

The fact is, no one addresses the world of an author with greater candor and authenticity than L. Ron Hubbard. Moreover, his pronouncements are timeless—every bit as pertinent to authorship in the nineties as when he originally fought his way into that vibrant pulp jungle. True, the paperback has long replaced the pulp, the

"...trying harder to make every word live and breathe."
– L. Ron Hubbard

advance-against-royalties, the penny-a-word, and the mass-market novelette is virtually no more. But the rest remains: the agents and editors, the markets and percentages, the scathing critics, the checkless Fridays, the "trying harder to make every word live and breathe." Then, too, the passion remains unchanged, "to write, write and then write some more. And never to allow weariness, lack of time, noise, or any other thing to throw me off my course."

In addition to instructional essays from his formative years, we include working notes on the shaping of the monumental *Battlefield Earth* and *Mission Earth* and the same again from the crafting of later screenplays. Also included are incidental remarks on life as a "manuscript factory," and much else following from the statement, "Somehow I got started in the writing business."

About the
Manuscript Factory

I STARTED OUT WRITING FOR THE PULPS, WRITING THE BEST I KNEW, WRITING FOR EVERY MAG ON THE STANDS, SLANTING AS WELL AS I COULD."

To which we might add: the earliest of his stories date from the summer of 1934, and a passing residence along the California coast just north of San Diego. He still suffered periodic chills from the touch of malaria contracted through the course of his Puerto Rican Mineralogical Expedition, and would later describe his financial predicament as classically grim—literally down to a last loaf of bread. Then, too, among the first submissions were several western sagas, soundly rejected as lacking authenticity—a particularly frustrating comment given those stories came straight from the heart of his Helena, Montana home. (While Max Brand, then undisputed king of the Wild West adventure, was actually a failed New York poet by the name of Frederick Schiller Faust, and he churned out his implausible six-shooter tales from the terrace of an Italian villa.)

As Ron further explains, however, with a half-a-million words shot-gunned out to a dozen markets, he actually saw sales from the start. The first to see print was a white-knuckled story of Asian intrigue entitled "The Green God." If the work is not especially memorable—a fairly

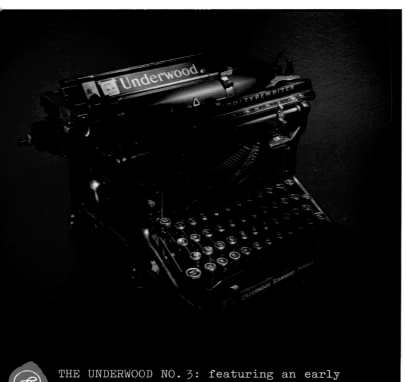

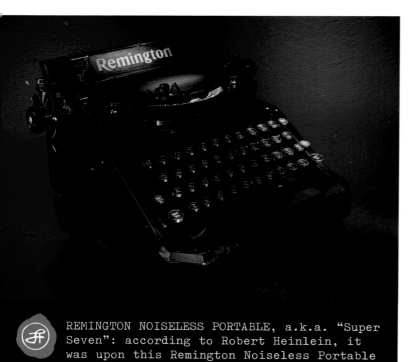

stock tale of a western intelligence officer in search of a stolen idol—it is nonetheless notable on at least one exceptional count: the young L. Ron Hubbard had, indeed, walked the gloomy streets of Tientsin, *and* in the company of a western intelligence officer—specifically, a Major Ian Macbean of the British Secret Service. Similarly, the young LRH had actually served aboard a working schooner not unlike those described in "The Pearl Pirate," had actually helped engineer a road through subtropical jungles as described in his highly atmospheric, "Sleepy McGee," while the chilling portrayal of voodoo rites in "Dead Men Kill" had been drawn from genuine adventures on Haiti.

The point, and one he would repeatedly stress: "You must have raw material. It gives you the edge on the field."

Still, that field was extremely competitive. Notwithstanding the great pulp appetite— approximately a million stories were said to have been published through the sixty-year pulp reign— the vast majority of those stories were actually authored by some three hundred hard-line professionals. Moreover, at a penny-a-word, those tales were pounded out pretty quickly. LRH friend and colleague Richard Sale (generally remembered for his "Daffy Dill" series and the Clark Gable vehicle *Strange Cargo*), would later tell of penning a story a day—three thousand words and more, every day. Then there was the legendary Arthur J. Burks, a.k.a. "Mr. Pulp," who regularly topped two million words a year—an astonishing feat for a typist, let alone a creative writer. While if the LRH rate of seventy thousand words a month (eventually a hundred thousand) seems rather less impressive, one must understand that wordage sprang from but three days a week at his Remington manual.

Yet even from the most accelerated prose comes a sense of something more enduring than the hammering of keys, "until I am finger worn to the second joint," as Ron so vividly phrased it. Later critics would speak of a "hard but brittle truth," and point to the work of pulpateer Horace McCoy and all he brought to French Existentialists André Gide and Jean-Paul Sartre. They would also speak of that

The genres spanned by L. Ron Hubbard included westerns, which have a remarkably provocative power and driving intensity of action that re-created for millions of readers the sense of the real Old West.

L. Ron Hubbard, center second row, with members of the New York chapter of the American Fiction Guild, of which he served as president in 1936.

As American Fiction Guild president, LRH devoted much time in assisting the neophyte author.

"unvarnished realism," and point to a Chandler and Hammett who, "took murder out of the Venetian case and dropped it into the alley," as Chandler himself would describe it. Then, too, they would point to an L. Ron Hubbard who was soon to accomplish the same for the supernatural novel, lifting it out of an unreal Gothic and weaving it into the fabric of any town USA.

The point here, as LRH so appropriately phrased it, and a point reiterated in one way or another by both Chandler and Hammett: "If you write insincerely, if you think the lowest pulp can be written insincerely and still sell, then you're in for trouble unless your luck is terribly good. And luck rarely strikes twice."

All this and more is the stuff of Ron's first instructional essay on the business of writing for the pulps. Aptly entitled "The Manuscript Factory," it dates from late 1935, or his formal admittance into the professional fold as President of New York's American Fiction Guild chapter. His residence stood at the 44th Street Hotel in Manhattan, augmented with a rented desk from the Wholey Office Equipment Company on Madison Avenue. Notwithstanding the continual clamor of "ten thousand taxi drivers," he continued to work much as before: "plotted the yarn in my sleep, rose and wrote it." Meals were generally taken at Rossoff's, unofficial Guild headquarters and watering hole for the likes of Lester "Doc Savage" Dent and

Walter "the Shadow" Gibson. In addition to regular duties—enlisting the New York City coroner to enlighten members on strange forms of murder— Ron's tenure as Guild president was largely devoted to the neophyte author. In particular, he sought their admittance to the Guild in the status of "novice," and otherwise worked to ease their entrance into the stables of a *Five Novels Monthly* or a *Thrilling Adventures*. He also passed on more than a few worthy names to his own agent extraordinaire, the wildly eccentric Ed Bodin who boasted $20,000 in annual sales, but still shared an office with a button broker and bill collector. Then, too, we find what is reprinted here for the education of all.

Considering what those "gentlemen of the craft" typically offered in the way of advice, Ron's "Manuscript Factory" is remarkably candid and enlightening. For the fact is, those two or three hundred hard-line pulpateers were generally a guarded lot, and particularly suspicious of those who would encroach upon their markets. There are accounts—possibly apocryphal, possibly not—of authors who actually came to blows over stolen plot twists. Then again, one hears of raging jealousies over half-a-penny advances in pay. In either case, here is what L. Ron Hubbard initially "learned about this writing business."

Factory

by L. RON HUBBARD

SO YOU WANT TO BE A PROFESSIONAL.

Or, if you are a professional, you want to make more money. Whichever it is, it's certain that you want to advance your present state to something better and easier and more certain.

Very often I hear gentlemen of the craft referring to writing as the major "insecure" profession. These gentlemen go upon the assumption that the gods of chance are responsible and are wholly accountable for anything which might happen to income, hours, or pleasure. In this way they seek to excuse a laxity in thought and a feeling of unhappy helplessness which many writers carry forever with them.

But when a man says that, then it is certain that he rarely, if ever, takes an accounting of himself and his work, that he has but one yardstick. You are either a writer or you aren't. You either make money or you don't. And all beyond that rests strictly with the gods.

I assure you that a system built up through centuries of commerce is not likely to cease its function just because your income seems to depend upon your imagination. And I assure you that the overworked potence of economics is just as applicable to this business of writing as it is to shipping hogs.

15

The Manuscript

You are a factory. And if you object to the word, then allow me to assure you that it is not a brand, but merely a handy designation which implies nothing of the hack, but which could be given to any classic writer.

Yes, you and I are both factories with the steam hissing and the chimneys belching and the machinery clanging. We manufacture manuscripts, we sell a stable product, we are quite respectable in our business. The big names of the field are nothing more than the name of Standard Oil on gasoline, Ford on a car, or Browning on a machine gun.

And as factories, we can be shut down, opened, have our production decreased, change our product, have production increased. We can work full blast and go broke. We can loaf and make money. Our machinery is the brain and the fingers.

And it is fully as vital that we know ourselves and our products as it is for a manufacturer to know his workmen and his plant.

Few of us do. Most of us sail blithely along and blame everything on chance.

Economics, taken in a small dose, are simple. They have to do with price, cost, supply, demand, and labor.

If you were to open up a soap plant, you would be extremely careful about it. That soap plant means your income. And you would hire economists to go over everything with you. If you start writing, ten to one, you merely write and let everything else slide by the boards. But your writing factory, if anything, is more vital than your soap factory. Because if you lose your own machinery, you can never replace it—and you can always buy new rolls, vats, and boilers.

The first thing you would do would be to learn the art of making soap. And so, in writing, you must first learn to write. But we will assume that you already know how to write. You are more interested in making money from writing.

It does no good to protest that you write for the art of it. Even the laborer who finds his chief pleasure in his work tries to sell services or products for the best price he can get. Any economist will tell you that.

You are interested in income. In net income. And "net income" is the inflow of satisfaction from economic goods, estimated in money, according to Seligman.[1]

I do not care if you write articles on knitting, children's stories, snappy stories, or gag paragraphs, you can still apply this condensed system and make money.

When you first started to write, if you were wise, you wrote anything and everything for everybody and sent it all out. If your quantity was large and your variety wide, then you probably made three or four sales.

1. Seligman: Edwin Robert Seligman (1861–1939), American economist; a former professor of political economy and finance at New York's Columbia University.

Factory

With the field thus narrowed, and you had say two types of markets to hammer at, you went ahead and wrote for the two. But you did not forget all the other branches you had first aspired to, and now and then you ripped off something out of line and sent it away and perhaps sold it and went on with the first two types regardless.

Take my own situation as an example—because I know it better than yours. I started out writing for the pulps, writing the best I knew, writing for every mag on the stands, slanting as well as I could.

I turned out about a half a million words, making sales from the start because of heavy quantity. After a dozen stories were sold, I saw that things weren't quite right. I was working hard and the money was slow.

Now it so happened that my training had been an engineer's. I leaned toward solid, clean equations rather than guesses, and so I took the list which you must have. Stories written, type, wordage, where sent, sold or not.

My list was varied. It included air-war, commercial air, western, western love, detective, and adventure.

On the surface, that list said that adventure was my best bet, but when you've dealt with equations long, you never trust them until you have the final result assured.

I reduced everything to a common ground. I took stories written of one type, added up all the wordage,[2] and set down the wordage sold. For instance:

DETECTIVE .... 120,000 words written

30,000 words sold

$$\frac{30,000}{120,000} = 25\%$$

ADVENTURE .... 200,000 words written

36,000 words sold

$$\frac{36,000}{200,000} = 18\%$$

According to the sale book, adventure was my standby, but one look at 18 percent versus 25 percent showed me that I had been doing a great deal of work for nothing. At a cent a word, I was getting $0.0018 for adventure, and $0.0025 for detective.

A considerable difference. And so I decided to write detectives more than adventures.

I discovered from this same list that, whereby I came from the West and therefore should know my subject, I had still to sell even one western story. I have written none since.

I also found that air-war and commercial air stories were so low that I could no longer afford to write them. And that was strange as I held a pilot's license.

Thus I was fooled into working my head off for little returns. But things started to pick up after that and I worked less. Mostly I wrote detective stories, with an occasional adventure yarn to keep up the interest.

But the raw materials of my plant were beginning to be exhausted. I had once been a police reporter and I had unconsciously used up all the shelved material I had.

And things started to go bad again, without my knowing why. Thereupon I took out my books, which I had kept accurately and up to date—as you should do.

Astonishing figures. While detective seemed to be my mainstay, here was the result.

2. Dating from 1935, "The Manuscript Factory," reflects LRH production and sales from his first professional year in the field. The bulk of stories referenced in this article date from 1933 and 1934, and effectively represent work from that period of "honing" for the market.

$$\text{DETECTIVE} \quad \frac{95{,}000 \text{ words sold}}{320{,}000 \text{ words written}} = 29.65\%$$

$$\text{ADVENTURE} \quad \frac{21{,}500 \text{ words sold}}{30{,}000 \text{ words written}} = 71.7\%$$

Thus, for every word of detective I wrote I received $0.002965 and for every adventure word, $0.00717. A considerable difference. I scratched my head in perplexity until I realized about raw materials.

I had walked some geography, had been at it for years, and thus, my adventure stories were beginning to shine through. Needless to say, I've written few detective stories since then.

About this time, another factor bobbed up. I seemed to be working very, very hard and making very, very little money.

But, according to economics, no one has ever found a direct relation between the value of a product and the quantity of labor it embodies.

A publishing house had just started to pay me a cent a word and I had been writing for their books a long time. I considered them a mainstay among mainstays.

Another house had been taking a novelette a month from me. Twenty thousand words at a time. But most of my work was for the former firm.

Dragging out the accounts, I started to figure up on words written for this and that, getting percentages.

I discovered that the house which bought my novelettes had an average of 88 percent. Very, very high.

And the house for which I wrote the most was buying 37.6 percent of all I wrote for them.

Because the novelette market paid a cent and a quarter and the other a cent, the average pay was: House A, $0.011 for novelettes on every word I wrote for them. House B, $0.00376 for every word I wrote for *them*.

I no longer worried my head about House B. I worked less and made more. I worked hard on those novelettes after that and the satisfaction increased.

That was a turning point. Released from drudgery and terrific quantity and low quality, I began to make money and to climb out of a word grave.

That, you say, is all terribly dull, disgustingly sordid. Writing, you say, is an art. What are you, you want to

know, one of these damned hacks?

No, I'm afraid not. No one gets a keener delight out of running off a good piece of work. No one takes any more pride in craftsmanship than I do. No one is trying harder to make every word live and breathe.

But, as I said before, even the laborer who finds his chief pleasure in his work tries to sell services or products for the best price he can get.

And that price is not word rate. That price is satisfaction received, measured in money.

You can't go stumbling through darkness and live at this game. Roughly, here is what you face. There are

The Manuscript

less than two thousand professional writers in the United States. Hundreds of thousands are trying to write—some say millions.

The competition is keener in the writing business than in any other. Therefore, when you try to skid by with the gods of chance, you simply fail to make the grade. It's a brutal selective device. You can beat it if

you know your product and how to handle it. You can beat it on only two counts. One had to do with genius, and the other with economics. There are very few men who sell and live by their genius only. Therefore, the rest of us have to fall back on a fairly exact science.

If there were two thousand soap plants in the country, and a million soap plants trying to make money, and you were one of the million, what would you do? Cutting prices, in our analogy, is not possible, nor fruitful in any commerce. Therefore you would tighten up your plant to make every bar count. You wouldn't produce a bar if you knew it would be bad. You'd think about such

things as reputation, supply, demand, organization, the plant, type of soap, advertising, sales department, accounting, profit and loss, quality versus quantity, machinery, improvements in product, raw materials, and labor employed.

And so it is in writing. We're factories working under terrific competition. We have to produce and sell at low cost and small price.

Labor, according to economics in general, cannot be measured in simple, homogenous units of time such as labor hours. And laborers differ, tasks differ, in respect to amount and character of training, degree of skill, intelligence, and capacity to direct one's work.

That for soap making. That also for writing. And you're a factory whether your stories go to *Satevepost*,[3] *Harper's*,[4] or an upstart pulp that pays a quarter of a cent on publication. We're all on that common level. We must produce to eat, and we must know our production and product down to the ground.

Let us take some of the above mentioned topics, one by one, and examine them.

SUPPLY AND DEMAND

You must know that the supply of stories is far greater than the demand. Actual figures tell nothing. You have only to stand by the editor and watch him open the morning mail. Stories by the truckload.

One market I know well, publishing five stories a month. Five long novelettes. Dozens come in every week from names which would make you sit up very straight and be very quiet. And only five are published. And if there's a reject from there, you'll work a long time before you'll sell it elsewhere.

That editor buys what the magazine needs, buys the best obtainable stories, from the sources she knows to

---

3. *Satevepost:* popular American national magazine, *Saturday Evening Post.*

4. *Harper's:* one of the oldest and most highly regarded periodicals of literary and political interest.

Factory

The Manuscript

be reliable. She buys impersonally as though she bought soap. The best bar, the sweetest smell, the maker's name. She pays as though she paid for soap, just as impersonally, but many times more dollars.

That situation is repeated through all the magazine ranks. Terrific supply, microscopic demand.

Realize now that every word must be made to count?

ORGANIZATION AND THE PLANT

Do you have a factory in which to work? Silly question, perhaps, but I know of one writer who wastes his energy like a canary wastes grain just because he has never looked at a house with an eye to an office. He writes in all manner of odd places. Never considers the time he squanders by placing himself where he is accessible. His studio is on top of the garage, he has no light except a feeble electric bulb, and yet he has to turn out seventy thousand a month. His nerves are shattered. He is continually going elsewhere to work, wasting time and more time.

Whether the wife or the family likes it or not, when the food comes out of the roller, a writer should have the pick and choice, say what you may. Me? I often take the living room and let the guests sit in the kitchen.

A writer needs good equipment. Quality of work is surprisingly dependent upon the typewriter. One lady I know uses a battered, rented machine which went through the world war judging by its looks. The ribbon will not reverse. And yet, when spare money comes in, it goes on anything but a typewriter.

Good paper is more essential than writers will admit. Cheap, unmarked paper yellows, brands a manuscript as a reject after a few months, tears easily, and creases.

Good typing makes a good impression. I have often wished to God that I had taken a typing course instead of a story writing course far back in the dim past.

Factory

RAW MATERIALS

Recently, a lady who once wrote pulp detective stories told me that, since she knew nothing of detective work, she went down to Center Street[5] and sought information. The detective sergeant there gave her about eight hours of his time. She went through the gallery, the museum, looked at all their equipment, and took copious notes.

And the sergeant was much surprised at her coming there at all. He said that in fifteen years, she was the third to come there. And she was the only one who really wanted information. He said that detective stories always made him squirm. He wished the writers would find out what they wrote.

And so it is with almost every line. It is so easy to get good raw materials that most writers consider it quite unnecessary.

Hence the errors which make your yarn unsalable. You wouldn't try to write an article on steel without at least opening an encyclopedia, and yet I'll wager that a fiction story which had steel in it would never occasion the writer a bit of worry or thought.

You must have raw material. It gives you the edge on the field. And no one tries to get it by honest research. For a few stories, you may have looked far, but for most of your yarns, you took your imagination for the textbook.

After all, you wouldn't try to make soap when you had no oil.

The fact that you write is a passport everywhere. You'll find very few gentlemen refusing to accommodate your curiosity. Men in every and any line are anxious to give a writer all the data he can use because, they reason, their line will therefore be truly represented. You're apt to find more enmity in not examining the facts.

Raw materials are more essential than fancy writing. Know your subject.

> *The competition is keener in the writing business than in any other. Therefore, when you try to skid by with the gods of chance, you simply fail to make the grade. It's a brutal selective device.*

TYPE OF WORK

It is easy for you to determine the type of story you write best. Nothing is more simple. You merely consult your likes and dislikes.

But that is not the whole question. What do you write and sell best?

A writer tells me that she can write excellent marriage stories, likes to write them, and is eternally plagued to do them. But there are few markets for marriage stories. To eat, she takes the next best thing—light love.

My agent makes it a principle never to handle a type of story which does not possess at least five markets. That way he saves himself endless reading, and he saves his writers endless wordage. A story should have at least five good markets because what one editor likes, another dislikes, and what fits here will not fit there. All due respect to editors, their minds change and their slant is never too ironbound. They are primarily interested in good stories. Sometimes they are overbought. Sometimes they have need of a certain type which you do not fill. That leaves four editors who may find the desired spot.

While no writer should do work he does not like, he must eat.

---

5. Center Street: address of police headquarters for lower Manhattan.

SALES DEPARTMENT

If you had a warehouse filled with sweet smelling soap, and you were unable to sell it, what would you do? You would hire a man who could. And if your business was manufacturing soap, your selling could not wholly be done by yourself. It's too much to ask. This selling is highly complex, very expensive.

Therefore, instead of wasting your valuable manufacturing time peddling your own manuscripts, why not let another handle the selling for you?

There's more than knowing markets to selling. The salesman should be in constant contact with the buyer. A writer cannot be in constant contact with his editors. It would cost money. Luncheons, cigars, all the rest. An agent takes care of all that and the cost is split up among his writers so that no one of them feels the burden too heavily.

An agent, if he is good, sells more than his 10 percent extra. And he acts as a buffer between you and the postman. Nothing is more terrible than the brown envelope in the box. It's likely to kill the day. You're likely to file the story and forget it. But the agent merely sends the yarn out again, and when it comes home, out again it goes. He worries and doesn't tell you until you hold the check in your hand.

The collaborating agent and the critic have no place here. They are advisors and doctors. Your sales department should really have no function except selling—and perhaps when a market is going sour, forward a few editorial comments without any added by your agent. This tends for high morale, and a writer's morale must always be high. When we started, we assumed that you already could write.

By all means, get an agent, and if you get one and he is no good to you, ditch him and try another. There are plenty of good agents. And they are worth far more than 10 percent.

ADVERTISING

Your agent is your advertising department. He can tell the editor things which you, out of modesty, cannot. He can keep you in the minds of the men who count.

But a writer is his own walking advertisement. His reputation is his own making. His actions count for more than his stories. His reliability is hard won and when won is often the deciding factor in a sale. Editors must know you can produce, that you are earnest in your attempt to work with them.

To show what actions can do, one writer recently made it a habit to bait an editor as he went out to lunch. This writer met this editor every day, forced his company on the editor and then, when they were eating, the writer would haul out synopsis after synopsis. The answer is, the writer doesn't work there anymore.

If a check is due, several writers I know haunt the office. It fails to hurry the check and it often puts an end to the contact when overdone. Many harry their editors for early decisions, make themselves nuisances in the office. Soon they stop selling there. Others always have a sob story handy.

Sob stories are pretty well taboo. It's hitting below the belt. And sob stories from writer to writer are awful. One man I know has wrecked his friendship with his formerly closest companions simply because he couldn't keep his troubles to himself. It's actually hurt his sales. You see, he makes more money than anyone I know, and he can't live on it. Ye gods, ALL of us have troubles, but few professionals use them to get checks or sympathy.

Reputation is everything.

It does not hurt to do extra work for an editor. Such as department letters.[6] Check it off to advertising. Answer all mail. Do a book for advertising. Write articles. Your name is your trademark. The better known the better sales.

6. letters to the editorial department of a magazine or newspaper.

The Manuscript

QUALITY VERSUS QUANTITY

I maintain that there is a medium ground for quantity and quality. One goes up, the other comes down.

The ground is your own finding. You know your best wordage and your best work. If you don't keep track of both, you should.

Write too little and your facility departs. Write too much and your quality drops. My own best wordage is seventy thousand a month. I make money at that, sell in the upper percentage brackets. But let me do twenty thousand in a month and I feel like an old machine, trying to turn over just once more before it expires. Let me do a hundred thousand in a month and I'm in possession of several piles of trips.[7]

The economic balance is something of your own finding. But it takes figures to find it. One month, when I was used to doing a hundred thousand per, I was stricken with some vague illness which caused great pain and sent me to bed.

For a week I did nothing. Then, in the next, I laid there and thought about stories. My average, so I thought, was shot to the devil. Toward the last of the month, I had a small table made and, sitting up in bed, wrote a ten thousand worder and two twenty thousand worders. That was all the work I did. I sold every word and made more in eight days than I had in any previous month.

That taught me that there must be some mean of average. I found it and the wage has stayed up.

There is no use keeping the factory staff standing by and the machinery running when you have no raw material.

7. trips: mistakes; blunders.

You can't sit down and stare at keys and wish you could write and swear at your low average for the month. If you can't write that day, for God's sakes don't write. The chances are, when tomorrow arrives, and you've spent the yesterday groaning and doing nothing, you'll be as mentally sterile as before.

Forget what you read about having to work so many hours every day. No writer I know has regular office hours. When you can't write, when it's raining and the kid's crying, go see a movie, go talk to a cop, go dig up a book of fairy stories. But don't sweat inactively over a mill. You're just keeping the staff standing by and the machinery running, cutting into your overhead and putting out nothing. You're costing yourself money.

Come back when you're fresh and work like hell. Two in the morning, noon, eight at night, work if you feel like it and be damned to the noise you make. After all, the

Factory

The Manuscript

people who have to hear you are probably fed by you and if they can't stand it, let them do the supporting. I take sprees of working at night, and then sleep late into the day. Once in the country farmers baited me every day with that unforgivable late slumber. It didn't worry me so much after I remembered that I made in a month what they made in a year. They think all writers are crazy, take the writer's license and make the best of it.

But don't pretend to temperament. It really doesn't exist. Irritation does and is to be scrupulously avoided.

When all the arty scribblers (who made no money) talked to a young lady and told her that they could not write unless they were near the mountains, or unless they had the room a certain temperature, or unless they were served tea every half-hour, the young lady said with sober mien, "Me? Oh, I can never write unless I'm in a balloon or in the Pacific Ocean."

One thing to remember. It seems to work out that your writing machine can stand just so much. After that the brain refuses to hand out plots and ideas.

It's like getting a big contract to sell your soap to the navy. You make bad soap, ruin the vats with a strong ingredient and let the finer machinery rust away in its uselessness. Then, when the navy soap contract ceases to supply the coffee and cakes, you discover that the plant is worthless for any other kind of product.

Such is the case of the writer who sees a big living in cheap fiction, turns it out to the expense of his vitality, and finally, years before his time, discovers that he is through. Only one writer of my acquaintance can keep a high word output. He is the exception, and he is not burning himself out. He is built that way.

But the rest of us shy away from too cheap a brand. We know that an advanced wage will only find us spending more. Soon, when the target for our unworthy efforts is taken down, we discover that we are unable to write anything else. That's what's meant by a rut.

As soon as you start turning out stories which you do not respect, as soon as you start turning them out wholesale over a period of time, as soon as your wordage gets out of control, then look for lean years.

To get anywhere at all in the business, you should turn out the best that's in you and keep turning it out. You'll never succeed in pulp unless you do, much less in the slicks.[8]

If you start at the lowest rung, do the best job of which you are capable, your product, according to economic law, will do the raising for you. Man is not paid for the amount of work in labor-hours, he is paid for the quality of that work.

8. slicks: magazines printed on glossy paper and usually having some artistic or intellectual pretensions.

Factory

IMPROVEMENT OF PRODUCT

With experience, your stories should improve. If they do not, then you yourself are not advancing. It's impossible not to advance, it's impossible to stand still. You must move, and you must slide back.

Take a story published a month ago, written six months ago. Read it over. If it seems to you that you could have done better, that you are doing better, you can sit back with a feline smile and be secure in the knowledge that you are coming up. Then sit forward and see to it that you do.

If you write insincerely, if you think the lowest pulp can be written insincerely and still sell, then you're in for trouble unless your luck is terribly good. And luck rarely strikes twice. Write sincerely and you are certain to write better and better.

So much for making soap and writing. All this is merely my own findings in an upward trail through the rough paper magazines. I have tested these things and found them to be true and if someone had handed them to me a few years ago, I would have saved myself a great deal of worry and more bills would have been paid.

Once, a professor of short story in a university gave me a course because I was bored with being an engineer. The course did not help much outside of the practice in writing. Recently I heard that professor address the radio audience on the subject, "This Business of Writing." It was not until then that I realized how much a writer had to learn. He knew nothing about the practical end of things and I told him so. He made me give a lecture to his class and they did not believe me.

But none of them, like you and I, have to make the bread and butter someway in this world. They had never realized that competition and business economics had any place whatever in the writing world. They

> *If you write insincerely, if you think the lowest pulp can be written insincerely and still sell, then you're in for trouble unless your luck is terribly good. And luck rarely strikes twice.*

were complacent in some intangible, ignorant quality they branded ART. They did not know and perhaps will someday find out, that art means, simply:

"The employment of means to the accomplishment of some end; the skillful application and adaptation to some purpose or use of knowledge or power acquired from Nature, especially in the production of beauty as in sculpture, etc.; a system of rules and established methods to facilitate the performance of certain actions."

They saw nothing praiseworthy in work well done. They had their hearts fixed on some goal even they did not understand. To them, writing was not a supreme source of expression, not a means of entertaining, not a means of living and enjoying work while one lived. If you wrote for a living, they branded you a hack. But they will never write.

Poor fools, they haven't the stamina, the courage, the intelligence, the knowledge of life's necessity, the mental capacity to realize that whatever you do in this life you must do well and that whatever talent you have is expressly given you to provide your food and your comfort.

My writing is not a game. It is a business, a hardheaded enterprise which fails only when I fail, which provides me with an energy outlet I need, which gives me the house I live in, which lets me keep my wife and boy. I am a manuscript factory but *not*—and damn those who so intimate it—an insincere hack, peddling verbal belly-wash with my tongue in my cheek. And I eat only so long as my factory runs economically, only so long as I remember the things I have learned about this writing *business.*

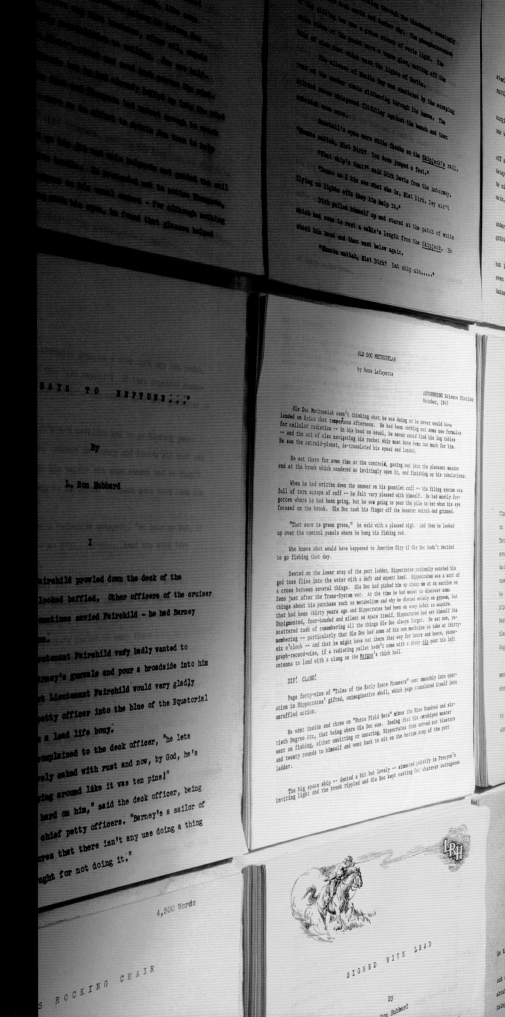

"You are a factory. And if you object to the word, then allow me to assure you that it is not a brand, but merely a handy designation which implies nothing of the hack, but which could be given to any classic writer."

- L. Ron Hubbard

Some of the thousands of manuscripts representing the more than 20 million words of fiction by L. Ron Hubbard.

The
Art of
Writing

NOTWITHSTANDING HIS HABITUAL WARNING ON THE PERILS OF

a New York residence—"Chances are a hundred to one that you

won't be able to turn out a line when the subway begins to saw

into your nerves"—by February, 1936, Ron had taken a basement

apartment in that perennial artistic enclave, Greenwich Village. By

all accounts, it was an interesting place with an ancient piano in the

sitting room and a fresco of pink cherubs (appropriately peeking

from clouds) on the ceiling. As we shall see, it was also routinely

filled with some fairly interesting characters.

There are dozens of telling anecdotes from Ron's stay in his King Street apartment: The afternoon he took control of a speeding subway in the name of research; the evening he slipped on an old tweed jacket and a porkpie hat for a black-tie reception at the Museum of Modern Art's first Picasso exhibition; the Paul Ernst mystery parties where guests were required to solve a mock murder, and talk of dastardly deeds finally grew so heated two neighboring matrons actually telephoned the police.

Of particular relevance to what follows here, however, were his various discussions with local artists on creativity in absolute terms—which is to say, aesthetics as a vastly misunderstood branch of philosophy. Those familiar with his final statement on the matter, *Art,* will recall mention of those discussions as when, "I used to buy breakfasts for Greenwich Village artists (which they ate hungrily,

This charcoal sketch of a 25-year-old L. Ron Hubbard by friend and artist Richard Albright hung above the editor's desk at Five Novels Monthly.

only stopping between bites to deplore my commercialism and bastardizing my talents for the gold that bought their breakfasts) . . ." Yet only passingly remarked upon is all that immediately followed from that line of inquiry, including a deepening and broadening of the L. Ron Hubbard story, and, in consequence, his steady ascension to the forefront of popular American fiction.

Critics would later speak in terms of a great pulp drama, replete with wonderfully complex characters in perfectly enticing settings: brooding traders in steamy Caribbean ports, embittered expatriots from the French Foreign Legion, and dark knights of the urban sprawl—all stuff of the LRH adventure through this period. Then, too, with his tale of a hapless passenger attempting to save the life of a girl who perished ten years earlier, we come upon the first of his supernatural mysteries in the 1936, "Death Flyer."

Ron's Greenwich Village "digs" at 40 King Street, advertised as a "garden basement" apartment.

Through his many detective and mystery novels readers experienced the hard-edged reality of police and crime.

What those tales inevitably brought him (quite in addition to ham and eggs for an ungrateful guest) is precisely the opposite of what that guest suggests with his talk of "dogeared magazines, each one forgotten the instant it is replaced on the stands by the next number." Indeed, explains speculative fiction master, Frederik Pohl, "the instant Ron's stories appeared on the newsstands, they became part of every fan's cultural heritage." Moreover, the fact those fans included "vapid stenogs, garbage collectors and housemaids"—to cite another stock gibe—is very much to the point of all L. Ron Hubbard represented as of 1936, and, for that matter, what the pulps in general represented as a literary force.

Finally, we might also consider this: when Ron speaks of an invitation to lecture on "the writing and marketing of short stories," he is referencing his eventual talks at Harvard University; while to appreciate his search for a central truth with which to explain the whole of this writing business "in one grand sweep," one need only turn to the pages of *Art*.

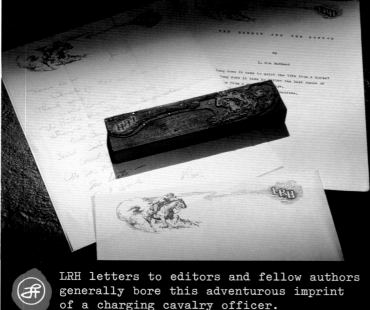

 LRH letters to editors and fellow authors generally bore this adventurous imprint of a charging cavalry officer.

"A writer needs good equipment," including this collection of ballpoint and fountain pens.

L. Ron Hubbard

L. Ron Hubbard
Author
c/o The Explorers Club, 46 East 70th Street
New York, New York 10021
Mailing Address: Post Office Box 29550
Los Angeles, California 90029

33

Art
vs.
Eats

by L. Ron Hubbard

It was midnight in the Village—or maybe three or four. The longhaired exponent of the moderns stabbed a slab of ham and somehow navigated the torturous course through uncombed shoals and to his mouth. He pointed his fork at me.

"But it's tripe! You know it's tripe. You aren't creating anything. You are taking a predetermined plot and garnishing it to suit the puerile taste of fatuous editors. You are shoveling out words as though they were so many beans. Ugh!" And he speared some scrambled eggs.

I think it far better to have been read and forgotten than never to have been read at all.

"My wares are read anyway," said I with wicked malice.

"Read! By whom pray tell? Taxi drivers and white wings[1] and vapid stenogs! By garbage collectors and housemaids . . ."

"And doctors and lawyers and merchants and thieves," I snapped.

"Why not? But what of it?" He emptied his fork into his bottomless cavern and again waved it before my nose. "What of it I say? You'll end up your days by never writing anything truly great. All you'll have to show for it is a stack of dogeared magazines, each one forgotten the instant it is replaced on the stands by the next number."

"Is there anything wrong with that?" I said. "Is it so different to lay away magazines than to stow unpublished manuscripts? When it comes to that my pro-nothing friend, I think it far better to have been read and forgotten than never to have been read at all."

"You dissemble. At least I am earnest. At least I am striving to write something truly great. At least my wares are not beneath my dignity and if those few I have published went unpaid they at least added their small bit to the true literature of the day. You fictioneers make my hair crawl. You prostitute a god-given gift for the sake of your stomachs. Mark my words," he said, ominously striving to put out my eyes with his useful fork, "you will live to regret it."

At the time I was quite amused for it was I who paid for that ration of ham and eggs he had so manfully mauled. For a long time afterwards I related the story to my brethren amid much applause. It was so funny, you see, for this shaggy half-bake to berate the source of the money which had paid for his

1. white wings: in reference to those working in New York City automats who served food and wore white long-sleeved coats.

much-needed meal. But through the din of laughter there still hovered a small doubt. What he had said was perfectly true. In fact it was so true that I was made very uneasy. To write millions and millions of words for the magazines was wonderful from a financial standpoint. But money isn't everything—or is it?

Now it so happens that this argument started long before two of the Pharaoh's chief poets fanned it into the raging flame which has carried it so far down the ages. On one hand there is the fellow who consoles himself with the thought that his work, unread, is too great; and on the other the man who says that though his work is not great, it is widely read.

In such a way do we all maunder. If we write "trash" we apologize for it. If we write "art" we bellicosely defend our right to starve. In such a way do all writers put themselves on the tilt field with their resulting wounds. Few indeed are the fellows who feel neither one way or the other about it.

This argument of art vs. eats is without foundation. It is a chimera. According to Voltaire, if one must argue, one must define his terms and, certainly, it is impossible to draw a line between art and trash for, where one ends and the other begins is wholly dependent upon the taste of the man who makes the distinction.

Unless, then, it is possible to discover some generality whereby these matters can be reconciled we will continue to stumble and stagger and apologize.

Quite accidentally I discovered what appears to be such a generality. Occasionally in this business of writing a fellow is called upon to stand up before aspirants to the profession and utter magic words. Rarely are the words very magic; usually the writer states that it is a fine business, that editors read manuscripts and that one has to produce to sell. Beyond that the wise speaker never ventures—for he would find himself as lonely as an eagle in the blue so far as understanding is concerned. Unless one has experienced editorial reactions, he cannot understand them. Unless one has been confronted with the woes of technique in their most Inquisitorial form, he cannot discourse upon relative merits. Unless one has a rather mysterious gift in the first place he cannot write at all. And so it goes.

But on this one particular occasion I was confronted with the epitome of impossibility. In so many words it was requested that I "talk for forty-five minutes and tell all about the writing and marketing of short stories." And as one could talk for forty-five years without getting deeper than the surface of the subject, the cue was for laughter. Anytime men find themselves confronted with impossibles, they laugh.

Still, the thing was a challenge. To tell *all* about the writing and selling of short stories in forty-five minutes would be an alp to climb. And that I refused to climb it irked me. I dislike the acknowledgment of impossibilities. It couldn't be done and it never had been done and it never would be done. . . . unless I could figure out some generality which would cover the whole subject in one grand sweep.

• • • • • • • • •

Notes on
Research

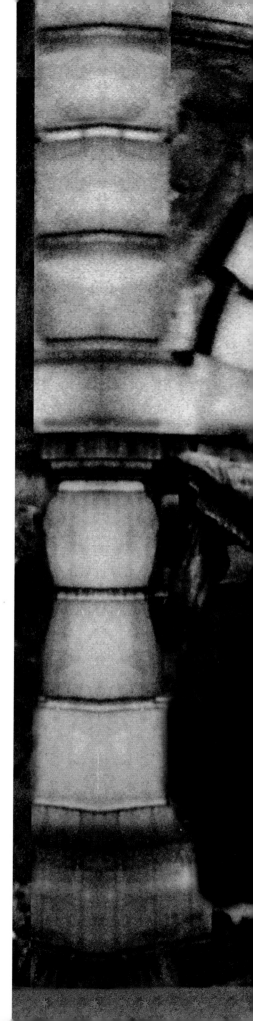

WITH HIS CONTINUED ADVANCE TO THE FOREFRONT OF POPULAR fiction, Ron found himself increasingly pressed for instructional lectures and articles—particularly those articles "in which there was a great deal of sound advice about writing and a number of examples," as he so simply described it. Among other topics eventually considered were the rarely discussed editorial canons: "The heroine must always be as pure as snowdrifts, unsullied, unsoiled, and the greatest worry is about the intentions of the big, bad, sneering, leering, rasping, grating, snarling villain." Then again, we find him offering a few choice remarks on the consequences of ignoring canons: "What courage it takes to break free! You stare at a vision of an empty cupboard. You seem to feel your toes peeping through your shoes, you already listen to the angry words of the landlord as he helps the sheriff toss your writing desk out into the street."

Of particular stress through LRH instructional articles, however, was the never-ending business of research.

The matter is not as obvious as one might imagine, and what Ron addresses has rarely been so plainly stated—namely, the actual process of conceiving a story. Of course, the dozen or more periodicals aimed at would-be wordsmiths of the day were forever offering "tips to inspire." The most interesting, if only as a curiosity, was the Plot Genie. Described as an "infallible" aid to the plotting of stories, the mail-order contraption featured two cardboard wheels with every conceivable literary contrivance matched with every conceivable stock character as in: the rancher's daughter enraptured with the lonesome drifter, or the disinherited stepson on the trail of lost treasure. Yet having plotted "three infallibles from that Genie," Ron explained, "I hated myself for days and days."

Buckskin Brigades, hardcover, 1937 (left);
Buckskin Brigades, paperback, 1987 (right).

What he instead provides is the actual stuff of literary grist—and not merely for that great pulp mill. For example, when LRH speaks of the "slim, forgotten fact," he is actually touching upon a critical element in much of what we regard as the most fascinating of stories, e.g., the slim forgotten history of Alexander Selkirk, inspiration for Daniel Defoe's *The Adventures of Robinson Crusoe*. Those works discussed here, as following from Ron's own examination of the slim and forgotten, are just as engaging.

The first, his "decidedly rare" and accurate portrayal of the Blackfeet, *Buckskin Brigades*, has enjoyed a long and respected history of reprint and review. The work has further received much acclaim from the Blackfeet themselves, whom a young Ron had known from the Montana of his youth and his ceremonial induction as a tribal Blood Brother at the age of six. Likewise memorable was his impelling adventure with Admiral Nelson on the Nile, "Mr. Tidwell—Gunner."

By way of a few ancillary notes: the Norvell Page encountered among the New York City Library stacks, was none other than Norvell "The Spider" Page, occasionally glimpsed through the Manhattan streets in a black cloak and sloping fedora—rather like his menacing hero. Those stories concerning the world's most dangerous professions were eventually known as the "Hell Job" series, and appeared in that original and most respected of all pulp periodicals, *Argosy*. In addition to what Ron relates on the shaping of "Test Pilot," he would elsewhere describe scaling rooftops with steeplejacks, plunging into a dark and chilled Puget Sound with navy divers and rolling bone-crushing logs with lumberjacks—all in the name of a continuing "search for research."

* * *

"Mr. Hubbard has reversed a time-honored formula and has given a thriller to which, at the end of every chapter or so, another paleface bites the dust . . . an enthusiasm, even a freshness and sparkle, decidedly rare in this type of romance."

— New York Times Book Review

The authenticity and perceptions in L. Ron Hubbard's adventure stories are drawn from his extensive travels and broad cultural research. His literature is part of an intensely and genuinely American idiom of literary expression and thought. His influence has stayed with us and does now, perhaps even more forcefully, shaping the direction of things to come. Between 1934 and 1950, L. Ron Hubbard wrote more than fifteen million words of fiction, in over two hundred classic publications. To span the many genres for which he wrote, he employed more than two dozen pseudonyms, some of which are: Winchester Remington Colt, Lt. Jonathan Daly, Capt. Charles Gordon, Bernard Hubbel, Michael Keith, Rene Lafayette, Legionnaire 148, Legionnaire 14830, Ken Martin, Scott Morgan, Lt. Scott Morgan, Kurt von Rachen, Barry Randolph, Capt. Humbert Reynolds and John Seabrook.

SEARCH FOR RESEARCH

BY L. RON HUBBARD

all of us want to sell more stories and write better ones. It is hard to believe that there exists a writer with soul so dead that he would not. But, from careful observation, I have come to the heart-breaking conclusion that while writers usually *want* to do this, they generally fail to try.

Writers are the laziest people on earth. And I know I'm the laziest writer. In common with the rest of the profession I am always searching for the magic lamp which will shoot my stories genie-like into full bloom without the least effort on my part.

This is pure idiocy on my part as I have long ago found this magic lamp, but not until a couple years ago did I break it out and use the brass polish to discover that it was solid gold.

> RESEARCH IS A HABIT WHICH IS ONLY ACQUIRED BY SHEER FORCE OF WILL. THE EASY THING TO DO IS GUESS AT THE FACTS — SO THINKS THE WRITER. WHEN, AS A MATTER OF FACTS, THE EASY THING TO DO IS GO *FIND* THE FACTS IF YOU HAVE TO TEAR A TOWN TO PIECES.

This lamp was so cobwebby and careworn that I am sure most of us have not looked very long at it in spite of its extreme age and in spite of the fact that it is eternally being called to our attention.

The name of this magic lamp is RESEARCH.

Ah, do I hear a chorus of sighs? Do I hear, "Hubbard is going to spring that old gag again." "What, another article on research? I thought LRH knew better."

In defense I instantly protest that I am neither the discoverer nor the sole exploiter of research. But I do believe that I have found an entirely new slant upon an ancient object.

In Tacoma a few months ago, I heard a writer sighing that he was having a hell of a time getting plots. This acute writing disease had eaten deeply into his sleep and bankbook. It had made him so alert that he was ruined as a conversationalist, acting, as he did, like an idea sponge. Hanging on and hoping but knowing that no ideas could possibly come his way.

As usual, I injected my thoughts into his plight—a habit which is bad and thankless.

I said, "Here's an idea. Why not go out and dig around in the old files at the library and the capitol at Olympia and find out everything you can on the subject of branding? There should be a lot of stories there."

He raised one eye and leered, "What? Do all that work for a cent and a half a word?"

And just to drive the idea home, I might remark that one day I happened into the New York public library. Crossing the file room I slammed into a heavy bulk and ricocheted back to discover I had walked straight into Norvell Page and he into me.

I gaped. "Page!"

"Hubbard!" he whispered in awed tones.

Solemnly we shook each other by the hand.

CHORUS: Well, this is the first time I ever saw a writer in a library!

These two instances should serve to illustrate the fact that research does not rhyme with writer no matter what kind of mill you pound.

Research is a habit which is only acquired by sheer force of will. The easy thing to do is guess at the facts—so thinks the writer. When, as a matter of facts, the easy thing to do is go *find* the facts if you have to tear a town to pieces.

Witness what happened last summer.

Staring me in the face were a stack of dangerous profession

stories which have since appeared in *Argosy*. At that time they were no more than started and I sighed to see them stretching forth so endlessly.

I chose "Test Pilot" as the next on the list and started to plot it. I thought I knew my aviation because the Department of Commerce[1] tells me so. Blithely, thinking this was easy, I started in upon a highly technical story without knowing the least thing about that branch of flying—never having been a test pilot.

For one week I stewed over the plot. For another week I broiled myself in the scorching heat of my self-accusation. Two weeks and nothing written.

Was I losing money fast!

There wasn't anything for it then. I had to find out something about test pilots.

Across the bay from my place in Seattle is the Boeing plant. At the Boeing plant there would be test pilots. I had to go!

And all for a cent and a half a word.

I went. Egdvedt, the Boeing president, was so startled to see a real live writer in the place that he almost talked himself hoarse.

Mitchell, the chief engineer, was so astounded at my ignorance that he hauled me through the plant until I had bunions the size of onions.

I sighed.

All for a cent and a half a word!

I went home.

1. In the 1930s the United States Department of Commerce was responsible for the testing and issuing of pilot licenses.

About that time it occurred to me that I used to write a lot for the *Sportsman Pilot* and, as long as I had the dope and data, I might as well fix the details in my head by writing them an article.

That done I suddenly saw a fine plot for my *Argosy* yarn and wrote that in a matter of a day and a half.

Two months went by. Arthur Lawson came in as editor of Dell and promptly remembered "Test Pilot" in *Argosy* and demanded a story along similar lines.

In two days I wrote that.

A month after that, Florence McChesney[2] decided that she needed a twenty thousand word flying story.

"Test pilot," says I, "do your stuff!"

Each and every one of those yarns sold first crack out. Article for the *Sportsman Pilot*, short for *Argosy*, short for *War Birds*, twenty thousand worder for *Five Novels*.

One day of research = several hundred bucks in stories.

This naturally made me think things over and, not being quite as foolish as editors think writers are,

I added up the account book and promptly went to work. Thus, the moral is yet to come.

On the dangerous profession stories which followed, I almost lost my life and broke my neck

trying to make them authentic. On each one I kept a complete list of notes and a list of plots which occurred to me at the time. There is enough writing material in that file to last me at least a year. It is the finest kind of copy because it is risky in the extreme, full of drama and high tension. I haven't any fears about mentioning this as any writer who is crazy enough to go down in diving suits and up in

spar trees[3] deserves all the help he can get.

But research does not end there and that is not the point of this article.

A short time ago I began to search for research on the theory that if I could get a glimmering of anything lying beyond a certain horizon I could go deep enough to find an excellent story.

I stopped doing what I used to do. There was a time when I expected a story to blaze up and scorch me all of its own accord. I have found, however, that there is a premium on divine fire and it is not very bright when used by a pulpateer. This gentleman has to write an immortal story about once every three days to keep eating.

On this plan I began to read exhaustively in old technical books, ancient travel books, forgotten literature. But not with the idea of cribbing. I wanted information and nothing else. I wanted

2. Editor of *Five Novels Monthly*.

3. spar trees: the tree-like arrangement of the round timbers used for extending sails on masts of multi-masted sailing vessels.

to know how the people used to think here, how the land lay there. Given one slim fact for a background, I have found it easy to take off down the channel of research and canal-boat out a cargo of stories.

In other words, I have no use for an obvious story idea as laid out in *Popular Mechanics* or *Forensic Medicine.* I want one slim, forgotten fact. From there a man can go anywhere and the story is very likely to prove unusual.

In one old volume, for instance, I discovered that there was such a thing as a schoolmaster aboard Nelson's ships of the line. That was a weird one. Why should Nelson want a schoolmaster?

Answer: Midshipmen.

When did this occur?

Answer: The Napoleonic Wars.

Ah, now we'll find out how those old ships looked. We'll discover how they fought, what they did.

And there was the schoolmaster during battle. Where?

In the "cockpit" helping hack off arms and legs.

Next lead indicated: Surgery during the Napoleonic Wars.

Wild guess in another allied field: Gunnery.

Again: Nelson.

A battle: On the Nile.

A ship or something strange about this battle: *L'Orient,* monster

French flagship which mysteriously caught fire and blew up throwing the weight of guns to Nelson.

Incidental discovery: "The Boy Stood on the Burning Deck" was written about the son of *L'Orient*'s skipper.

Back to midshipmen, the King's Letter Boys: They were hell on wheels, arrogant, ghastly urchins being trained as officers.

> I WANTED INFORMATION AND NOTHING ELSE. I WANTED TO KNOW HOW THE PEOPLE USED TO THINK HERE, HOW THE LAND LAY THERE. GIVEN ONE SLIM FACT FOR A BACKGROUND, I HAVE FOUND IT EASY TO TAKE OFF DOWN THE CHANNEL OF RESEARCH AND CANAL-BOAT OUT A CARGO OF STORIES.

And with all this under my mental belt I girded up my mental loins. Complete after a few days of search I had "Mr. Tidwell, Gunner," which appeared in *Adventure.*

All that because I chanced to find there was a schoolmaster aboard Nelson's ships of the line.

This is now happening right along because I haven't let the idea slide as my laziness dictated I should.

The final coup d'état arrived last winter.

Boredom had settled heavily upon me and I sat one evening

staring vacantly at a shelf of books. They were most monotonous. Whole sets stretched out along the shelves with very little change in color or size. This annoyed me and I bent forward and took one out just to relieve the regularity.

It proved to be Washington Irving's *Astoria,* his famous epic of the fur trading days.

It had never been brought home to me that Irving had written such a book and to find out why, I promptly started to read it. The result was, of course, a fur trading story. But the method of arriving at this story was so indirect that it merits a glance.

Irving only served to call to my attention that I was out in the fur trading Northwest and that I had certainly better take advantage of the history of the place.

I roved around, found very little because I had no direct starting point. I went to the Encyclopaedia Britannica to discover a bibliography of such source books and started out again to ferret them out.

All these books were contemporary with fur trading days, all of them written, of course, by white men. But everywhere I kept tripping across the phrases, "The Warlike Blackfeet." "The Bloodthirsty Blackfeet."

This finally penetrated my thick skull. I did not like it because I thought I knew something about the Blackfeet.

Were they as bad as they were represented?

Into the records. The real records. Into Alexander Henry's journal. Into this and out of that until I had a stack of material higher than my desk.

And then I capped the climax by locating a young chap in Seattle who happens to be a blood brother of the Blackfeet. Lewis and Clark's Journal contained about five pages concerning the circumstances which surrounded the killing of a Blackfoot brave by Lewis.

The way this suddenly shot down the groove is remarkable to remember. The Hudson's Bay Company, the Nor'Westers, the Blackfeet, John Jacob Astor . . . The story pieces dovetailed with a click.

Coupled with years of experience in the northwest, these hundred sources jibed to make the story.

The result was *Buckskin Brigades,* a novel being put out this summer by Macaulay.

Buckskin Brigades came to life because I happened to be bored enough one evening to sit and stare at a line of books on a shelf.

This account of researching is not complete unless I mention a certain dogging phobia I have and which I suspect is deeply rooted in most of us.

H. Bedford Jones mentioned it long ago and I did not believe him at the time. But after rolling stacks of it into the mags, I know that BJ was right as a check.

He said that it was hard for a person to write about the things he knew best.

This gives rise to an ancient argument which says pro and con that a writer should write about the things he knows.

> I BELIEVE THAT THE ONLY WAY I CAN KEEP IMPROVING MY WORK AND MY MARKETS IS BY BROADENING MY SPHERE OF ACQUAINTANCESHIP WITH THE WORLD AND ITS PEOPLE AND PROFESSIONS.

Witnesseth: I was born and raised in the West and yet it was not until last year that I sold a couple westerns. And I only sold those because somebody said I couldn't.

Know ye: The Caribbean countries know me as El Colorado and yet the only Caribbean stories I can write are about those countries which I have touched so briefly that I have only the vaguest knowledge of them and am therefore forced to depend upon researching the books and maps for my facts.

Hear ye: I wrote fine Hollywood stories until I came down here and worked in pictures. I wrote one while here and the editor slammed it back as a total loss.

There are only a few exceptions to this. I have been able to cash in heavily upon my knowledge of North China because the place appealed to me as the last word in savage, romantic lore. The last exception seems to be flying stories, though after flying a ship I can't write an aviation story for a month.

The final proof of this assertation came in connection with my Marine Corps stories. Most of my life I have been associated with the Corps one way or another in various parts of the world and I should know something about it.

But I have given up in dark despair.

"He Walked to War" in *Adventure* was branded as technically imperfect.

"Don't Rush Me" in *Argosy,* another marine story, elicited anguished howls of protest.

And yet if there is any story in the world I should be qualified to write, it is a marine story.

These are my woes. The reason for them is probably very plain to everyone. But I'll state my answer anyway.

A man cannot write a story unless he is deeply interested in it. If he thinks he knows a subject then he instantly becomes careless with his technical details.

The only way I have found it possible to sidetrack these woes is by delving into new fields constantly, looking everywhere for one small fact which will lead me on into a story field I think I'll like.

This is not very good for a writer's reputation, they tell me. A writer, it is claimed, must specialize to become outstanding. I labored trying to build up a converse reputation, hoping to be known as a writer of infinite versatility.

I did not know until two years ago that the specializing writer is *non persona grata* with an editor. Jack Byrne, for instance, rebuilt *Argosy* with variety as a foundation. And once I heard Bloomfield[4] sigh that he wished some of his top-notchers would stop sending him the same background week in and week out.

Maybe I am right, possibly I am wrong.

But I believe that the only way I can keep improving my work and my markets is by broadening my sphere of acquaintance-ship with the world and its people and professions.

4. Bloomfield, Howard: editor of *Adventure* magazine.

S U S P

For all later talk of L. Ron Hubbard as a "legendary master of science fiction's golden age," to quote another critic of the genre, let us never forget him as first and foremost an author of adventure. After all, not only did he cut his literary teeth on those tales of bold men in desperate straits, but the great bulk of the LRH catalog undisputedly falls within that realm of high adventure.

In the main, and as noted, a fair quantity of that adventure was actually drawn from the author's own fairly adventurous life. To cite another typical example: his 1936, "Sky Birds Dare," tells of a glider pilot's harrowing flight to prove the military worth of a powerless aircraft; while an undergraduate at George Washington University, Ron had not only held local records for sustained powerless flight, but was generally known for aerial antics that "made women scream and strong men weep." Yet there was another factor attendant to the LRH acclaim in the likes of Western Action, Argosy and Thrilling Detective, and that is the stuff of his 1937 "Suspense."

In a later assessment of what made pulp action so utterly memorable, an editor of the era would speak of an emphasis on minute detail, subtlety of emotion and a plausibility no matter how implausible the setting or circumstances. Then, too, one hears much talk of the classic pulp pacing and what those from Black Mask so succinctly described as "swift movement and action." (While for a comparative sense of what Ron terms that "dragging agony of suspense," one

need only examine a climatic sequence from a Hammett, Chandler or Erle Stanley Gardner of "Perry Mason" fame. But in either case, nowhere does one find such a careful analysis of what rivets a reader to a page, "tensely wondering which of two or three momentous things is going to happen first."

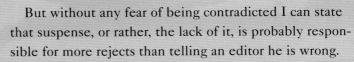

by L. Ron Hubbard

Next to checks, the most intangible thing in this business of writing is that quantity "Suspense."

It is quite as elusive as editorial praise, as hard to corner and recognize as a contract writer.

But without any fear of being contradicted I can state that suspense, or rather, the lack of it, is probably responsible for more rejects than telling an editor he is wrong.

You grab the morning mail, find a long brown envelope. You read a slip which curtly says, "Lacks suspense."

Your wife starts cooking beans, you start swearing at the most enigmatic, unexplanatory, hopeless phrase in all that legion of reject phrases.

If the editor had said, "I don't think your hero had a tough enough time killing Joe Blinker," you could promptly sit down and kill Joe Blinker in a most thorough manner.

But when the editor brands and damns you with that first cousin to infinity, "Suspense," you just sit and swear.

Often the editor, in a hurry and beleaguered by stacks of manuscripts higher than the Empire State, has to tell you something to explain why he doesn't like your wares. So he fastens upon the action, perhaps. You can tell him (and won't, if you're smart) that your action is already so fast that you had to grease your typewriter roller to keep the rubber from getting hot.

Maybe he says your plot isn't any good, but you know doggone well that it is a good plot and has been a good plot for two thousand years.

Maybe, when he gives you those comments, he is, as I say, in a hurry. The editor may hate to tell you you lack suspense because it is something like B.O.—your best friends won't tell you.

But the point is that, whether he says that your Mary Jones reminds him of the *Perils of Pauline*, or that your climax is flat, there's a chance that he means suspense.

Those who have been at this business until their fingernails are worn to stumps are very often overconfident of their technique. I get that way every now and then, until something hauls me back on my haunches and shows me up. You just forget that technique is not a habit, but a constant set of rules to be frequently refreshed in your mind.

And so, in the scurry of getting a manuscript in the mail, it is not unusual to overlook some trifling factor which will mean the difference between sale and rejection.

This suspense business is something hard to remember. You know your plot (or should, anyway) before you write it. You forget that the reader doesn't. Out of habit, you think plot is enough to carry you through. Sometimes it won't. You have to fall back on none-too-subtle mechanics.

Take this, for example:

He slid down between the rocks toward the creek, carrying the canteens clumsily under his arm, silently cursing his sling. A shadow loomed over him.

"Franzawi!" screamed the Arab sentinel.

There we have a standard situation. In the Atlas. The hero has to get to water or his wounded legionnaires will die of thirst. But, obviously, it is very, very flat except for the slight element of surprising the reader.

Surprise doesn't amount to much. That snap ending tendency doesn't belong in the center of the story. Your reader knew there were Arabs about. He knew the hero was going into danger. But that isn't enough. Not half.

Legionnaire Smith squirmed down between the rocks clutching the canteens, his eyes fixed upon the

> *Next to checks, the most intangible thing in this business of writing is that quantity "Suspense."*

bright silver spot which was the water hole below. A shadow loomed across the trail before him. Hastily he slipped backward into cover.

An Arab sentinel was standing on the edge of the trail, leaning on his long gun. The man's brown eyes were turned upward, watching a point higher on the cliff, expecting to see some sign of the besieged legionnaires.

Smith started back again, moving as silently as he could, trying to keep the canteens from banging. His sling-supported arm was weak. The canteens were slipping.

He could see the sights on the Arab's rifle and knew they would be lined on him the instant he made a sound.

The silver spot in the ravine was beckoning. He could not return with empty canteens. Maybe the sentinel would not see him if he slipped silently around the other side of this boulder.

He tried it. The man remained staring wolfishly up at the pillbox fort.

Maybe it was possible after all. That bright spot of silver was so near, so maddening to swollen tongues. . . .

Smith's hand came down on a sharp stone. He lifted it with a jerk.

A canteen rattled to the trail.

For seconds nothing stirred or breathed in this scorching world of sun and stone.

Then the sentry moved, stepped a pace up the path, eyes searching the shadows, gnarled hands tight on the rifle stock.

Smith moved closer to the boulder, trying to get out of sight, trying to lure the sentry toward him so that he could be silently killed.

The canteen sparkled in the light.

A resounding shout rocked the blistered hills.

"Franzawi!" cried the sentinel.

The surprise in the first that a sentinel would be there and that Smith was discovered perhaps made the reader blink.

The dragging agony of suspense in the latter made the reader lean tensely forward, devour the page, gulp . . .

Or at least, I hope it did.

But there's the point. Keep your reader wondering which of two things will happen (i.e., will Smith get through or will he be discovered) and you get his interest. You focus his mind on an intricate succession of events, and that is much better than getting him a little groggy with one swift sock to the medulla oblongata.

That is about the only way you can heighten drama out of melodrama.

It is not possible, of course, to list all the ways this method can be used. But it is possible to keep in mind the fact that suspense is better than fight action.

And speaking of fight action, there is one place where Old Man Suspense can be made to work like an Elkton marrying parson.[1]

Fights, at best, are gap fillers. The writer who introduces them for the sake of the fight itself and not for the effects upon the characters is a writer headed for eventual oblivion even in the purely action books.

> ## *The dragging agony of suspense…made the reader lean tensely forward, devour the page, gulp…*

Confirmed by the prevailing trend, I can state that the old saw about action for the sake of action was right. A story jammed and packed with blow-by-blow accounts of what the hero did to the villain and what the villain did to the hero, with fists, knives, guns, bombs, machine guns, belaying pins, bayonets, poison gas, strychnine, teeth, knees, and calks is about as interesting to read as the *Congressional Record* and about twice as dull. You leave yourself wide open to a reader comment, "Well, what of it?"

But fights accompanied by suspense are another matter.

Witness the situation in which the party of the first part is fighting for possession of a schooner, a girl or a bag of pearls. Unless you have a better example of trite plotting, we proceed. We are on the schooner. The hero sneaks out of the cabin and there is the villain on his way to sink the ship. So we have a fight:

Jim dived at Bart's legs, but Bart was not easily thrown. They stood apart. Jim led with his left, followed through with his right. Black Bart countered the blows. Bone and sinew cracked in the mighty thunder of conflict. . . . Jim hit with his right. . . . Bart countered with a kick in the shins. . . .

There you have a masterpiece for wastebasket filing. But, believe it, this same old plot and this same old fight look a lot different when you have your suspense added. They might even sell if extracted and toned like this:

Jim glanced out of the chart room and saw Black Bart. Water dripping from his clothes, his teeth bared, his chest heaving from his long swim, Bart stood in a growing pool which slid down his arms and legs. In his hand he clutched an axe, ready to sever the hawser and release them into the millrace of the sweeping tide. . . .

1. reference to Elkton, Maryland where marriages were performed with little formality and legal requirements.

This is Jim's cue, of course, to knock the stuffing out of Black Bart, but that doesn't make good reading nor very much wordage, for thirty words are enough in which to recount any battle as such, up to and including wars.

So we add suspense. For some reason Jim can't leap into the fray right at that moment. Suppose we add that he has these pearls right there and he's afraid Ringo, Black Bart's henchman, will up and swipe them when Jim's back is turned. So first Jim has to stow the pearls.

This gets Bart halfway across the deck toward that straining hawser which he must cut to wreck the schooner and ruin the hero.

Now, you say, we dive into it. Nix. We've got a spot here for some swell suspense. Is Black Bart going to cut that hawser? Is Jim going to get there?

Jim starts. Ringo hasn't been on his way to steal the pearls but to knife Jim, so Jim tangles with Ringo, and Black Bart races toward the hawser some more.

Jim's fight with Ringo is short. About like this:

Ringo charged, eyes rolling, black face set. Jim glanced toward Bart. He could not turn his back on this charging demon. Yet he had to get that axe.

Jim whirled to meet Ringo. His boot came up and the knife sailed over the rail and into the sea. Ringo reached out with his mighty hands. Jim stepped through and nailed a right on Ringo's button. Skidding, Ringo went down.

Jim sprinted forward toward Bart. The blackbearded Colossus spun about to meet the rush, axe upraised.

Now, if you want to, you can dust off this scrap. But don't give it slug by slug. Hand it out, thus:

The axe bit down into the planking. Jim tried to recover from his dodge. Bart was upon him, slippery in Jim's grasp. In vain Jim tried to land a solid blow, but Bart was holding him hard.

"Ringo!" roared Bart. "Cut that hawser!"

Ringo, dazed by Jim's blow, struggled up. Held tight in Bart's grasp, Jim saw Ringo lurch forward and yank the axe out of the planking.

"That hawser!" thundered Bart. "I can't hold this fool forever!"

Now, if you wanted that hawser cut in the first place (which you did, because that means more trouble and the suspense of wondering how the schooner will get out of it) cut that hawser right now before the reader suspects that this writing business is just about as mechanical as fixing a Ford.

Action suspense is easy to handle, but you have to know when to quit and you have to evaluate your drama and ladle it out accordingly.

Even in what the writers call the psychological story you have to rely upon suspense just as mechanical as this.

Give your reader a chance to wonder for a while about the final outcome.

There is one type of suspense, however, so mechanical that it clanks. I mean foreshadowing.

To foreshadow anything is weak. It is like a boxer stalling for the bell. You have to be mighty sure that you've got something outstanding to foreshadow, or the reader will nail up your scalp.

It is nice to start ominously like this:

I knew that night as I sloshed through the driving rain that all was not well. I had a chilly sense of foreboding as though a monster dogged my steps. . . .

If I only had known then what awaited me when the big chimes in the tower should strike midnight, I would have collapsed with terror …

Very good openings. Very, very good. Proven goods, even though the nap is a bit worn. But how many times have writers lived up to those openings? Not very many.

You get off in high, but after you finish you will probably tear out these opening paragraphs—even though Poe was able to get away with this device. Remember the opening of "The Fall of the House of Usher"? You know, the one that goes something like this: "Through the whole of a dark and dismal afternoon."

That is foreshadowing. However, few besides Poe have been able to get away with suspense created by atmosphere alone.

One particular magazine makes a practice of inserting a

> *To foreshadow anything is weak. It is like a boxer stalling for the bell.*

foreshadow as a first paragraph in every story. I have come to suspect that this is done editorially because the foreshadow is always worse than the story gives you.

It's a far cry from the jungles of Malaysia to New York, and there's a great difference between the yowl of the tiger and the rattle of the L,[2] but in the city that night there stalked the lust of the jungle killers and a man who had one eye. . . .

I have been guilty of using such a mechanism to shoot out in high, but I don't let the paragraph stand until I am pretty doggone sure that I've got everything it takes in the way of plot and menace to back it up.

If you were to take all the suspense out of a story, no matter how many unusual facts and characters you

had in it, I don't think it would be read very far.

If you were to take every blow of action out of a story and still leave its suspense (this is possible, because I've done it) you might still have a fine story, probably a better story than before.

There is not, unhappily, any firm from which you can take out a suspense insurance policy. The only way you can do it is to make sure that the reader is sitting there tensely wondering which of two or three momentous things is going to happen first. If you can do that, adroitly to some of those manuscripts which have come bouncing back, they may be made to stay put.

2. L: an *el*evated railway once in existence in New York.

57

Despite all the pulps offered as a passport to far-flung adventure, one persistent link to ordinary life remained: the single column advertisement on the front and back pages. Why those advertisements so often tended towards the oddball or salacious is a difficult question, but apparently followed from yet another pulp-paper myth—that the typical reader was both low-class and gullible. In fact, the pulps pervaded the whole of American society. To wit: while future Nobel laureate Sinclair Lewis provided editorial assistance to Adventure, *readers included none other than President Franklin Roosevelt. But in either case, the first and final pages remained filled with ads for false teeth, eczema ointment and the rest of what Ron describes in his wry commentary on "The Pulp Paper Puzzle."*

The *PulpPaper* PUZZLE

by L. RON HUBBARD

IF YOU'RE BASHFUL AND EASILY EMBARRASSED, PLEASE LAY THIS THING ASIDE.

If I had good sense, I wouldn't write this or even mention it because, as a cautious friend once said, "Many a man has been noosed for less." But if I'm doing wrong, please keep in mind that this is *not* a slam against editors, only an attempt to help them and myself and our brethren. And it isn't a slam against publishers because publishers can't do anything about it either, at the moment. And it isn't a slam against pulps because I like pulps and I write pulps and I think many of them are vastly underrated as literature.

I speak, and God help me, about pulp advertising, and I speak about it in the terms two thousand writers speak about it and I think it's about time somebody said something, and right now I happen to be all burned up.

In a recent issue, a novelette of mine was carried over into the back of one of our pulps. Right at the point where the heroine was being very shy and where the hero was being good and pure and saving her virtue, I saw this ad:

THE FORBIDDEN SECRETS OF SEX ARE DARINGLY REVEALED

Away with false modesty. At last a famous doctor has told all the secrets of sex in frank, daring language. No prudish beating about the bush, no veiled hints, but TRUTH. . . .

Imagine my gentle heroine's embarrassment when she was confronted with that!

It has been said before and often that the pulps have to have advertising of some kind, but no one has bothered to explain to me just why a group with half a million guaranteed circulation has to take that kind.

And somebody has said someplace that these ads have to appear somewhere and there's really nothing wrong with the ads, either. They're just out of place.

Pulps, bless 'em, print the cleanest stories which appear on the stands as a whole. Pulps have taboos which are the run-of-the-mill in a lot of slick[1] offices.

1. slick: having to do with magazines printed on glossy paper and usually having some artistic or intellectual pretensions.

Take the hero. He has to be red-blooded, plenty tough, virile, clean-minded, active, pure, good, and a model any boy might be glad to emulate.

It follows, then, that the people reading the pulps want to read about fine fellows. These people buy the pulps because of the stories. Why, then, must an advertising man insist that the pulp paper book is the place for such an ad.

Maybe I'm dumb, I dunno. But the whole pulp code is built upon one fact. One book, one dish. The taboos run the same, the stories run in the same channel. Every editorial effort is based upon that one thing.

Then why doesn't the same method apply to the ads?

Two and two, in my day, made four. In pulps ads they make me sick.

I am generally very broad-minded. In fact, my mind, they tell me, is simply a wide-open space.

I read the pulps for amusement, the same as anyone else, not entirely for business. And when I read about red-blooded men I am seeking escape and more escape. I want to be right out there in the jungle knocking the hell out of the natives with the hero. I feel like I'm big and tough, too, and that I can climb mountains, get wounded, climb mountains and still be so virile that I can still climb more mountains. I want to be like the hero and these heroes aren't too far drawn at that.

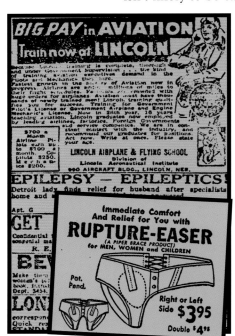

But in the midst of my reading, the page turns, right while I'm in my glory of being tough with Mr. Hero, and I read:

STOP YOUR RUPTURE WORRIES

LEARN ABOUT MY PERFECTED RUPTURE INVENTION.

Swell thought while I'm busy being tough.

But, they tell me, ads pay writers indirectly. That's why I can't understand it. If ads pay me at all, then why the devil don't they pay me big.

In the waiting room of a big pulp publisher I heard an ad man—and God knows they have their troubles too—selling a man on an inch spread.

"We have, in these books," said the ad man—poor devil—"A guaranteed circulation of one million. Your ad will be run in each book and it will reach all these people. Now if you don't get results, you'll get your money back, and if you don't get the guaranteed circulation, you'll get a rebate."

Well, I guess he had to tell that guy something, but it's puzzled me ever since. One million circulation for that string of books. There's less duplication than you think. A western reader snarls and snaps at your hand when you offer him an air book. And a love pulp reader isn't likely to be caught reading horror stories.

But now, with one million circulation, which is what a few slicks boast, and a lot of them far less, a slick goes out and gets swell drawings and full color and good copy. They advertise soap and furniture and cars and electric iceboxes of fine make. They get plenty of money for those ads, otherwise they'd have to get more money for their books.

I dunno, I'm just a writer. I'm not supposed to worry my head about such things. But my pulp rates aren't anything to brag about, and neither are yours so don't sneer, and sometimes I get funny ideas about word rates, thinking in my dumb way that after all, my wife deserves to eat *once* in a while.

And so we come back to the ads and the pulps. The pulps—so one well-known publisher whose name would surprise you—are known for their advertising, and are damned for it. He said that was the main trouble with the pulps—this big man with his million circulation—and that the ads held the pulps back.

But I haven't seen him doing anything about it in his books.

Maybe he can't do anything about it. Certainly there is no agency to handle pulp ads, although one has vaguely given a statement upon this to . . .

Let's take the grand old man of the pulps, the book which is greater than all the other books and which has a fine type of readers.

Fine, convincing stories, no woman interest. A book I'd like to have my boy read when he grows up.

The copy here, opened at random, begins with:

THE FIRST GIRL I EVER LIKED AND THESE PIMPLES HAD TO COME!

Swell ad, but it so happens that this book, this granddaddy of pulps, has no woman interest whatever and it got there through lack of it. Its readers want nothing at all to do with women. They are seekers beyond the horizon and their thoughts are far away, in lands where tom-toms mutter and where a man can be a man and has to be a man to live—and to hell with the dames.

The company which runs this ad is a fine firm. It runs the same ad in the comic strips and I dare say the thing might work there. But there seems to be a gap, a lack of . . .

Next!

This is more to the point in this book, as it happens to deal with far lands:

BE A DETECTIVE. EXPERIENCE UNNECESSARY.

Another:

BE A DETECTIVE. FOLLOW THIS MAN.

Again:

BE A DETECTIVE.

We'll take a good western book which has no woman interest at all. A book which is read by a lot of people I know who are very intelligent people. I like the book,

too. But it so happens that the wide-open-space appeal is capped by:

PILES, DON'T BE CUT.

By:

BE A DETECTIVE.

And in the midst of a column which says that the next issue will contain Explosive Action, we read:

DON'T DYNAMITE KIDNEYS.

I mean these things are not in step somehow.

It's not that people shouldn't be warned that you must

WAKE UP YOUR LIVER BILE

it's that the reader wants to forget all about it, escape it or he wouldn't be reading the book. After all, when a specter of liver bile is hanging over your head and you want to get away from it all . . .

The detective book is fine in its choice of ads. Detectives are notorious for their disguises and:

FALSE TEETH, 60 DAY TRIAL.

Going on from the defendant teeth we are informed that:

KIDNEYS CAUSE MUCH TROUBLE.

Of course this is perfectly all right and I'm not making fun of the pulps at all. I'm trying to defend them. It isn't the editor's fault that his book is filled with such stuff, and it isn't the advertising man's either. Both these boys are on the spot and they would do something about it I know if they could. Of course . . .

When my stories are published I don't feel bad about having them appear on wood pulp paper. Why should I? I'm doing a sincere, honest task. I am nothing more or less than an entertainer. But I cringe a little when my

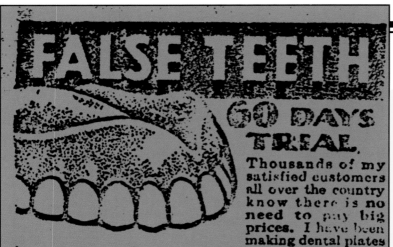
friends read them because, invariably, along about the climax, this jumps up:

PROSTATE GLAND WEAKNESS.

Hell's bells, fellow craftsmen, we wouldn't mention it in polite society if we had it, would we?

Now let's take a cruise into the love pulp field.

I have seen an odd survey of the readers of one of the best of these mags. Surprised, I learned that the readers are not added up to an average age. I thought that high-school people and gum-chewing stenos ate them up. I was wrong.

The people that read love pulp are anywhere from sixteen to sixty in any walk of life. They are respectable matrons, schoolteachers, cashiers, wives, and the girl who lives in the swank apartment down the hall with her mom and pop. A varied, intelligent audience, when you come to think of it, and if they aren't, then you're slamming America.

You and I have their equals in our own friends. They are the ladies who buy and buy and buy some more. They wear the latest and they use the best lipstick and they influence the old man when he buys his car, and they use soap and electric iceboxes, and what the devil do they care about:

IF YOU DO NOT ADD AT LEAST THREE INCHES TO YOUR CHEST, IT WON'T COST YOU ONE CENT!

MOLD A MIGHTY CHEST AND AMAZE YOUR FRIENDS.

And then, remembering that this is a love pulp, we read:

A TIP GOT BILL A GOOD JOB

TRAIN IN SPARE TIME AT HOME

FOR RADIO WORK.

This is presented in the light that a tip comes from a girl. He wins the job and the jane and everybody is happy, and the idea is that the girl will read it and tell Bill and they won't have any more money worries and he won't be out of a job and they can feed the kiddies.

When the whole doggone book is busy putting the man in romance, stressing the beauty of a cozy nest for two, this doesn't seem to jibe somehow. The gals will probably shudder when they read it and say, "So that's the price of marriage." Anticlimax for ten happy-ending stories when *he* gives *her* the ring.

With no alibi to qualify its presence in a woman's book:

A MONEY-MAKING OPPORTUNITY FOR MEN OF CHARACTER.

BE A TRAVELING SALESMAN FOR US.

ENDLESS OPPORTUNITIES FOR THE RIGHT MAN.

And also:

MR. SALESMAN! WHAT'S WRONG?

That's subtle, that one is. But we go on, still in the love book, read by all these nice people as that survey testifies.

GET ON AVIATION'S PAYROLL.

Also very subtle, if you know what I mean. Fact is, I know the chap who runs this last outfit and he's a prince. But he's paying a little money in this book for that ad and I don't think he could spot it anywhere else, and I don't think he'd want to pay a big price for it.

And still in the love pulp, we have:

FOLLOW THIS MAN!

Not bad, I guess, but it's about being a detective.

But when we run into this one, we wonder.

FOREST JOBS

HUNT, TRAP, CABIN.

Dear, dear me, am I blushing about all this. But I think the ladies must love:

SEE ABOUT MY TEETH BEFORE ORDERING ELSEWHERE

FALSE TEETH AT LOWEST PRICES.

And of course this too is right in line:

SAVE ON TIRES.

These things are all flattering, I suppose, but take a look at this:

QUIT WHISKEY.

This is another one I get the creeps reading in this book devoted to sweet, gentle adoration:

PROSTATE GLAND WEAKNESS.

and

EPILEPSY—EPILEPTICS

And this, of course, has a definite place in the book:

STRONG MEN AT ALL TIMES HAVE USED DUMBBELLS TO GAIN THEIR GREAT STRENGTH.

And again:

GET RID OF YOUR PIMPLES.

I assure you it goes on and on, and I'm taking all the ads as I come to them. How about:

ITCHING STOPPED QUICKLY.

and:

JOBLESS MEN, READ THIS!

All in a love mag too. Well, well, well.

By this time you have probably stopped reading or you're gagged beyond all help. But just listen at me a second. This is the stuff which appears beside your story and mine. This is the thing our readers have to read the instant they open the book the first time. A fine introduction.

We see "Joe Writer's smashing story, 'Bilgewater Bill's Mistake' " and then, right against that announcement we'll see:

DO YOU SUFFER FROM PSORIASIS??

ECZEMA,

ACNE CURED.

I can never quite reconcile myself and tell myself that the reader of that announcement won't go through life associating Joe Writer with a pimply face.

But I grow lengthy over this. Actually I cannot quite bring myself to write up three or four of these ads for fear that I'd blush for days. I leave them out. You can find them in your own pulps.

Other ads I have omitted are those dealing with time-payment jewelry, which is okay, with typewriters (showing that typewriter people have sense) and with tap-dancing. Nor do I mention these fake offers of information where you expect one thing and get another and a request for more dough.

In connection with that last, the funniest thing I have seen this month is a column in a detective mag which exposes rackets for the readers. This month the columnist is exposing a certain concern and right there in the ad across the page is the whole copy, word for word, which he is exposing.

I omit, too, the pen-pal clubs and old money. I omit the one saving grace—those swell-looking cigarette ads on the back and a couple furniture ads.

But those are all. Just those, no more. I have the field covered.

The argument against big companies advertising in the pulps is twofold. The big company doesn't want to be in such companionship, and the returns from these pulp ads is not sufficient. Good arguments against it.

But here is what I'm driving at. You and I are writers. We are supposed to know nothing about such things. But if you have snickered or blushed while reading this article, then please realize that your friend the reader does exactly the same thing. He's no different from us, except that we're probably a little dumber than he is.

I am taking a load upon myself in writing this at all. Don't think I shoot off my face for my health because it isn't at all healthy.

Up in the advertising offices of the Big Five,[1] angry advertising men, I suppose, will take this in to the boss and swear at it. And then word will come through the office that every time L. Ron Hubbard has a story in *Dashing Stories*, or in *Gun-Slingers*, or in *Gun Novels*, the circulation goes down. Plese don't give us no more Hubbard nohow.

The men have a right to be sore about it. In one way

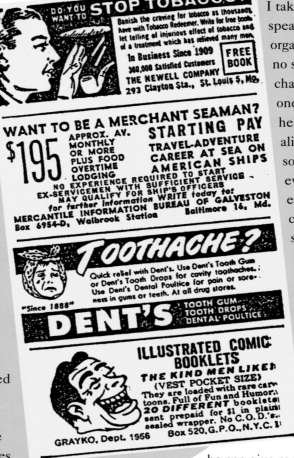

such things as this take the bread out of the mouths of babes (I've got two, thanks).

But nobody will boycott a chap who tries like hell to make the magazine pay. Well, indirectly though it seems, I'm trying to up my own rates and your rates and the profit on the book.

This idea is not original with me. I take no credit for it and I am not speaking with authority for any organization. However, I've named no solutions. That's for the other chap, that's the business of this one outfit of which I speak, helping writers and publishers alike. One of these days the solution will be advanced and everybody will be very happy, especially you and I with a big check in the pocket instead of a small check.

Publishers look with suspicion upon writers and their organization. They think the purpose they have in mind is forcing more money per word out of the tottering editorial budget.

That doesn't happen to be the truth. If a writer can boost sales of a book, and if he can give real, material help, and if he has any ideas what makes the dough come in, then he should be allowed to speak his piece in peace. That he is not, is true to many a man's everlasting sorrow and it probably will be to mine.

But somebody has to say something about this first and I'm saying it right here. Soon, if you and you and you give it moral support, we will see all the big advertising agencies paying attention and—what is more important—cold cash to the pulps.

The first step has been taken. I am not the crusader, only the recorder. Since starting this article I have been told that I can tell you this. I wanted to be sure.

Through the American Fiction Guild, the key man of a large advertising firm has become interested in pulp

1. reference to the publishers Popular, Standard, Munsey, Dell, Street & Smith.

ads. The Guild offered to conduct a reader survey, offered to bring all publishers together. The Guild is meeting with some success in this and even those publishers who have not bothered to take the course through the Guild (which is all the same to the outfit) are gradually working out the problem.

They are afraid, those publishers, (and this is strictly my idea) that their big accounts will be jerked away from them by other houses. Each house is working separately under this delusion, failing to see this evident fact.

National advertising will become a concrete fact, raising profit and rates, only when every good pulp on the stands, whether it be published by POPULAR, STANDARD, MUNSEY, DELL, or STREET & SMITH, banishes this foolish copy forever and does away with the only bugaboo which is keeping national advertising from their pages.

All houses have to pull together in this. No dog eat dog about it.

The Guild's part in the affair was merely starting the ball rolling and the program is already becoming an accomplished fact.

It takes nerve to go at this thing. One house has already gone at it and I haven't permission to mention its name. It found, in the first real survey it ever conducted, that their readers averaged thirty-five years of age. Not fourteen to nineteen.

This house banished all the ads it could (though a lot of their copy is still bad because of contracts which they cannot break). For a long time advertising brought in nothing although specialists were hired.

But just when this house was about to throw up its hands, several good, national accounts fell their way. They are on the road. Gradually they'll put a little more dignity into the space and quit this comic-strip attack advertisers think they have to use in pulp.

Several accounts, big money, and the other houses will soon be following. This first house will realize more money on their space when other houses do follow suit.

And so, from the stand of the crusader, I become a prosaic reporter.

But the fight is not won, it has to go on. Someday we hope that you won't be ashamed of the pages in which your yarns appear. They're good yarns, they're excellent books. Men with intelligence read them and thrill to them.

Things are still slow. But shortly you'll see steam roaring out of the kettle and we'll be in better shape, all of us.

MAGIC OUT OF A HAT

BY L. RON HUBBARD

Given the sheer quantity of copy required for survival in that menacing pulp jungle, authors of the realm were frequently hardpressed for ideas. The highly stylized, and thus comparatively slow, Raymond Chandler regularly cannibalized his own work if only to keep himself fed at a penny-a-word. While reasoning that what's sauce for the gander will also serve the goose, others tell of recycling plots from arctic adventures as Sahara tales, and aerial twists as deep-sea thrillers. Even more to the point here, the aforementioned Richard Sale tells of drawing inspiration from whatever object in his office seemed to suggest a story: an empty whiskey bottle, a dented cigarette lighter, a handful of nickels. Similarly, we come to A. J. Burks' common wastebasket and Ron's "Magic Out of a Hat."

WHEN ARTHUR J. BURKS TOLD ME TO put a wastebasket upon my head, I knew that one of us—probably both—was crazy. But Burks has a winning way about him, and so I followed his orders and thereby hangs a story. And what a story!

You know of course how all this pleasant lunacy started. Burks bragged openly in *Writer's Digest* that he could give six writers a story apiece if they would just name an article in a hotel room. So six of us took him up on it and trooped in.

The six were Fred "Par" Painton, George "Sizzling Air" Bruce, Norvell "Spider" Page, Walter "Curly-top" Marquiss, Paul "Haunted House" Ernst, and myself. An idiotic crew, if I do say it, wholly in keeping with such a scheme to mulch editors with alleged stories. I spied a wastebasket in Burks' room and told him to plot me a story around it.

He ordered me to put a wastebasket on my head, told me that it reminded me of a *kubanka* (Ruski lid, if you aren't a Communist) and ordered me to write the story. I won't repeat here the story he told me to write. It was clean, that's about all you can say for it—(although that says a great deal coming from an ex-Marine).

This wastebasket didn't even look faintly like a *kubanka*. A *kubanka* is covered with fur, looks like an ice-cream cone minus its point, and is very nice if you're a Ruski. I wrote the story up that same night. Don't go wrong and find Art's article to see how he would do it. I'll show you the *right way*.

Burks told me to write about a Russian lad who wants his title back and so an American starts the wheels rolling, which wheels turn to gun wheels or some such drivel, and there's a lot of flying in the suggestion, too. Now I saw right there that Art had headed me for a cheap action story not worth writing at all. He wanted to do some real fighting in it and kill off a lot of guys.

But I corrected the synopsis so I didn't have to save more than the

Russian Empire and I only bumped about a dozen men. In fact, my plot was real literature.

The conversation which really took place (Burks fixed it in his article so he said everything) was as follows:

BURKS: I say it looks like a hat. A *kubanka*.

HUBBARD: It doesn't at all. But assuming that it does, what of it?

BURKS: Write a story about it.

HUBBARD: Okay. A lot of guys are sitting around a room playing this game where you throw cards into a hat and gamble on how many you get in. But they're using a fur wastebasket for the hat.

BURKS: A fur wastebasket? Who ever heard of that?

HUBBARD: You did just now. And they want to know about this fur wastebasket, so the soldier of fortune host tells them it's a *kubanka* he picked up, and he can't bear to throw it away although it's terrible bad luck on account of maybe a dozen men getting bumped off because of it. So he tells them the story. It's a "frame" yarn, a neat one.

BURKS: But you'll make me out a liar in my article.

HUBBARD: So I'll make you a liar in mine.

So I started to plot the story. This hat is a very valuable thing, obviously, if it's to be the central character in a story. And it is a central character. All focus is upon it.

> # THE OTHERS EYED THE OBJECT AND STUART TURNED IT AROUND IN HIS HANDS, GAZING THOUGHT-FULLY AT IT.

Next I'll be writing a yarn in second person.

Anyway, I was always intrigued as a kid by an illustration in a book of knowledge. Pretty red pictures of a trooper, a fight, a dead trooper.

You've heard the old one: For want of a nail the shoe was lost, for want of a shoe the horse was lost, for want of a horse the rider was lost, for want of a rider the message was lost, for want of a message the battle was lost, and all for the want of a horseshoe nail.

So, it's not to be a horseshoe nail

but a hat that loses a battle or perhaps a nation. I've always wanted to lift that nail plot and here was my chance to make real fiction out of it. A hat. A lost empire.

Pretty far apart, aren't they? Well, I'd sneak up on them and maybe scare them together somehow. I made the hat seem ominous enough and when I got going, perhaps light would dawn. Here we go:

"That's a funny looking hat," I remarked.

The others eyed the object and Stuart turned it around in his hands, gazing thoughtfully at it.

"But not a very funny hat," said Stuart, slowly. "I don't know why I keep it around. Every time I pick it up I get a case of the jitters. But it cost too much to throw away."

That was odd, I thought. Stuart was a big chap with a very square face and a pocketful of money. He bought anything he happened to want and riches meant nothing to him. But here he was talking about cost.

"Where'd you get it?" I demanded.

Still holding the thing, still looking at it, Stuart sat down in a big chair. "I've had it for a long, long time but I don't know why. It

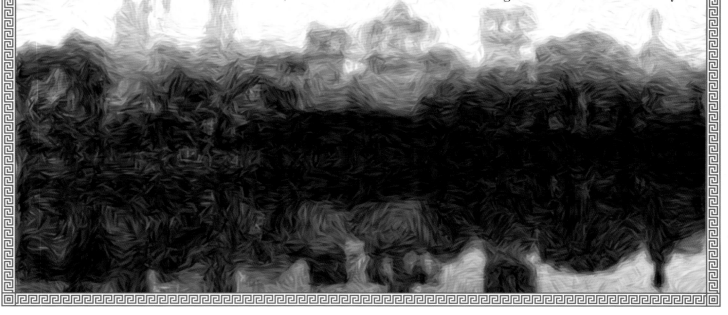

spilled more blood than a dozen such hats could hold, and you see that this could hold a lot.

Something mournful in his tone made us take seats about him. Stuart usually joked about such things.

Well, there I was. Stuart was telling the story and I had to give him something to tell. So I told how he came across the hat.

This was the world war, the date was July 17th, 1918; Stuart was a foreign observer trying to help Gajda, the Czech general, get Russia back into fighting shape. Stuart is in a clearing.

. . . and the rider broke into the clearing.

From the look of him he was a Cossack. Silver cartridge cases glittered in the sun and the fur of his *kubanka* rippled in the wind. His horse was lathered, its eyes staring with exertion. The Cossack sent a hasty glance over his shoulder and applied his whip.

Whatever was following him did not break into the clearing. A rifle shot roared. The Cossack sat bolt upright as though he had been a compressed steel spring. His head went back, his hands jerked, and he slid off his horse, rolling when he hit the ground.

I remember his *kubanka* bounced and jumped and shot in under a bush . . .

Feebly he motioned for me to come closer. I propped him up

> . . . I CAN'T HAVE MY HERO KILLED, NATURALLY, AS THIS IS A FIRST-PERSON STORY, SO I PASS THE TORCH TO ANOTHER . . .

and a smile flickered across his ashy face. He had a small arrogant mustache with waxed points. The blackness of it stood out strangely against the spreading pallor of his face.

"The . . . *kubanka* . . . Gajda." That was all he would ever say. He was dead.

Fine. The *kubanka* must get to General Gajda. Here I was, still working on the horseshoe nail and the message.

The message, the battle was lost. The message meant the *kubanka*.

But how could a *kubanka* carry a message? Paper in the hat? That's too obvious. The hero's still in the dark. But here a man has just given his life to get this hat to the Czechs and the hero at least could carry on, hoping General Gajda would know the answer.

He was picking up the message he knew the hat must carry. He had killed three men in a rifle battle at long range in an attempt to save the Cossack. There's suspense and danger for you. A white man all alone in the depths of Russia during a war. Obviously somebody else is going to get killed over this hat. The total is now four.

I swore loudly into the whipping wind. I had no business getting into this fight in the first place. My duty was to get back to the main command and tell them Ekaterinburg was strongly guarded. Now I had picked up the Cossack's torch. These others had killed the Cossack. What would happen to me?

So my story was moving along after all. The fact that men would die for a hat seems so ridiculous that when they do die it's horrible by contrast, seemingly futile.

But I can't have my hero killed, naturally, as this is a first-person

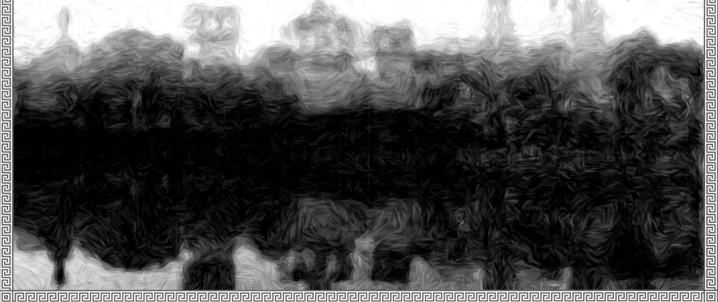

story, so I pass the torch to another, one of the hero's friends, an English officer.

This man, as the hero discovers later, is murdered for the *kubanka* and the *kubanka* is recovered by the enemy while the hero sleeps in a hut of a muzjik beside the trail.

The suspense up to here and ever farther is simple. You're worried over the hero, naturally. And you want to know, what's better, why a hat should cause all this trouble. That in itself is plenty reason for writing a story.

Now while the hero sleeps in the loft, three or four Russian Reds come in and argue over the money they've taken from the dead Englishman, giving the hero this news without the hero being on the scene.

The hat sits in the center of the table. There it is, another death to its name. Why?

So they discover the hero's horse in the barn and come back looking for the hero. Stuart upsets a lamp in the fight, the hut burns but he cannot rescue the hat. It's gone.

Score nine men for the hat. But this isn't an end in itself. Far from it. If I merely went ahead and said that the hat was worth a couple hundred kopeks, the reader would get mad as hell after reading all this suspense and sudden death. No, something's got to be done about that hat, something startling.

What's the most startling thing I

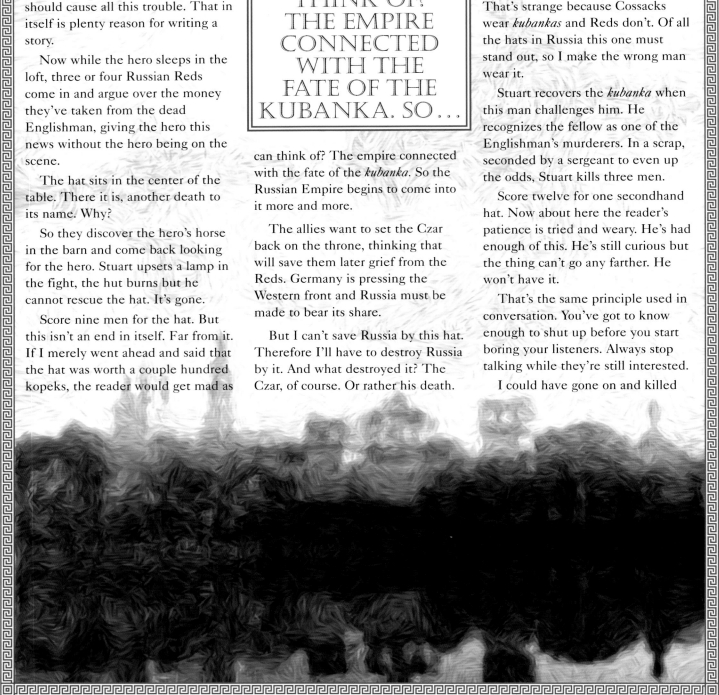

WHAT'S THE MOST STARTLING THING I CAN THINK OF? THE EMPIRE CONNECTED WITH THE FATE OF THE KUBANKA. SO . . .

can think of? The empire connected with the fate of the *kubanka*. So the Russian Empire begins to come into it more and more.

The allies want to set the Czar back on the throne, thinking that will save them later grief from the Reds. Germany is pressing the Western front and Russia must be made to bear its share.

But I can't save Russia by this hat. Therefore I'll have to destroy Russia by it. And what destroyed it? The Czar, of course. Or rather his death.

The Czech army moves on Ekaterinburg, slowly because they're not interested so much in that town. They could move faster if they wanted. This for a feeling of studied futility in the end.

They can't find the Czar when they get there. No one knows where the Czar is or even if he's alive.

This must be solved. Stuart finds the hat and solves it.

He sees a Red wearing a *kubanka*. That's strange because Cossacks wear *kubankas* and Reds don't. Of all the hats in Russia this one must stand out, so I make the wrong man wear it.

Stuart recovers the *kubanka* when this man challenges him. He recognizes the fellow as one of the Englishman's murderers. In a scrap, seconded by a sergeant to even up the odds, Stuart kills three men.

Score twelve for one secondhand hat. Now about here the reader's patience is tried and weary. He's had enough of this. He's still curious but the thing can't go any farther. He won't have it.

That's the same principle used in conversation. You've got to know enough to shut up before you start boring your listeners. Always stop talking while they're still interested.

I could have gone on and killed

every man in Russia because of that hat and to hell with history.

History was the thing. People know now about the Czar, when and where he was killed and all the rest. So that's why I impressed dates into the first of the story. It helps the reader believe you when his own knowledge tells him you're right. And if you can't lie convincingly, don't ever write fiction.

Now the hero, for the first time (I stressed his anxiety in the front of the story) has a leisurely chance to examine this hat. He finally decides to take the thing apart, but when he starts to rip the threads he notices that it's poorly sewn.

This is the message in the hat, done in Morse code around the band:

"Czar held at Ekaterinburg, house of Ipatiev. Will die July 18. Hurry."

Very simple, say you. Morse code, old stuff. But old or not, the punch of the story is not a mechanical twist.

The eighteenth of July has long past, but the hero found the hat on the seventeenth. Now had he been able to get it to Gajda, the general's staff could have exhausted every possibility and uncovered that message. They could have sent a threat to Ekaterinburg or they could have even taken the town in time. They didn't know, delayed, and lost the Russian Czar and perhaps the nation.

Twelve men, the Czar and his family, and an entire country dies because of one hat.

Of course the yarn needs a second punch, so the hero finds the jewels of the Czar in burned clothing in the woods and knows that the Czar is dead for sure and the Allied cause for Russia is lost.

The double punch is added by the resuming of the game of throwing cards into this hat.

After a bit we started to pitch the cards again. Stuart sent one sailing across the room. It touched the hat and teetered there. Then, with a flicker of white, it coasted off the side and came to rest some distance away, face up.

We moved uneasily. I put my cards away.

The one Stuart had thrown, the one which had so narrowly missed, was the king of spades.

Well, that's the "Price of a Hat." It sold to Leo Margulies' *Thrilling Adventures* magazine of the Standard Magazines, Inc., which, by the way, was the magazine that bought my first pulp story. It will appear in the March issue, on sale, I suppose, in February. Leo is pretty much of an adventurer himself and without boasting on my part, Leo knows a good story when he sees it. In a letter to my agent accepting my story, Leo Margulies wrote: "We are glad to buy Ron Hubbard's splendid story 'The Price of a Hat.' I read the *Digest* article and am glad you carried it through."

Art Burks is so doggoned busy these days with the American Fiction Guild and all, that you hardly see anything of him. But someday I'm going to sneak into his hotel anyway, snatch up the smallest possible particle of dust and make him make me write a story about that. I won't write it but he will. I bet when he sees this, he'll say:

"By golly, that's a good horror story." And sit right down and make a complete novel out of one speck of dust.

Anyway, thanks for the check, Art. I'll buy you a drink, at the next luncheon. What? Heck, I didn't do *all* the work!

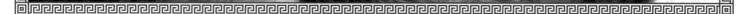

Among the more revealing notes on this business of writing, and of particular significance to anyone who has faced a fickle editor, is Ron's *"How to Drive a Writer Crazy."*

Although undated, it would seem to fit the infamously difficult John W. Campbell—forever bombarding authors with contradictory ideas and frightening more than a few into mental paralysis, "by showing his vast knowledge of a field, . . . especially on subjects where nothing is known anyway." In either case, what Ron describes is not merely amusing; it is also the ruin of many a young literary talent.

HOW to Drive a Writer Crazy

by L. Ron Hubbard

1. When he starts to outline a story, immediately give him several stories just like it to read and tell him three other plots. This makes his own story and his feeling for it vanish in a cloud of disrelated facts.

2. When he outlines a character, read excerpts from stories about such characters, saying that this will clarify the writer's ideas. As this causes him to lose touch with the identity he felt in his character by robbing him of individuality he is certain to back away from ever touching such a character.

3. Whenever the writer proposes a story, always mention that his rate, being higher than other rates of writers in the book, puts up a bar to his stories.

4. When a rumor has stated that a writer is a fast producer, invariably confront him with the fact with great disapproval as it is, of course, unnatural for one human being to think faster than another.

5. Always correlate production and rate, saying that it is necessary for the writer to do better stories than the average for him to get any consideration whatever.

6. It is a good thing to mention any error in a story bought, especially when that error is to be editorially corrected as this makes the writer feel that he is being criticized behind his back and he wonders just how many other things are wrong.

7. Never fail to warn a writer not to be mechanical as this automatically suggests to him that his stories are mechanical and, as he considers this a crime, wonders how much of his technique shows through and instantly goes to much trouble to bury mechanics very deep—which will result in laying the mechanics bare to the eye.

8. Never fail to mention and then discuss budget problems with a writer as he is very interested.

9. By showing his vast knowledge of a field, an editor can almost always frighten a writer into mental paralysis, especially on subjects where nothing is known anyway.

10. Always tell a writer plot tricks as they are not his business.

The Golden Age

IT WILL PROBABLY BE BEST TO RETURN TO THE DAY IN 1938 WHEN I FIRST ENTERED THIS FIELD, THE DAY I MET JOHN W. CAMPBELL, JR., A DAY IN THE VERY DAWN OF WHAT HAS COME TO BE KNOWN AS THE GOLDEN AGE OF SCIENCE FICTION."

In addition to what is told of that day in Ron's frequently quoted introduction to *Battlefield Earth*, let us provide the following: John W. Campbell was then twenty-eight years old, and not quite a graduate of the Massachusetts Institute of Technology. (He had failed to master the requisite languages, and so finally earned a Bachelor of Science degree from Duke University.) He had nonetheless proven himself a capable enough author of the genre with a spaceship driven epic, appropriately entitled *The Machine* series. In suggesting Campbell had originally resisted publishing L. Ron Hubbard and Arthur J. Burks, however, Ron is touching upon a highly significant point of science fiction history, i.e., Campbell was *not* initially that *force majeure* behind the genre's golden age; it was the far less scientifically minded F. Orlin Tremaine, who had then held an editorial directorship over Street & Smith's *Astounding,* and had indeed invited LRH and A. J. Burks into the fold because he wished an infusion of *character*-driven stories. Or as Ron himself explains, "he was going to get *people* into his stories and get something going besides *machines.*" Then, too, in describing himself as initially diffident and, actually, "quite ignorant" of that science fiction realm, Ron is touching upon another highly significant point: that is, what initially fueled that golden age was not, as is so frequently argued, a John Campbell vision of brave new technological wonders penned by a stable of techno-authors from MIT and Cal Tech. No, what fueled the new science fiction was the same stuff fueling all great pulp fiction— which is to say, all we have thus far examined in "this business of writing."

Nevertheless, and despite all inherent differences, L. Ron Hubbard

and John W. Campbell soon set forth beneath the banner of a new science fiction. The first LRH offering, and not one Campbell would have necessarily published had F. Orlin Tremaine left him unfettered, was entitled "The Dangerous Dimension." In contrast to the typical Campbell setting amidst gleaming spaceports off the rings of Saturn, that most startling "dangerous dimension" opens in the utterly prosaic office of Yamouth University's Professor Henry Mudge. Nor do we find the usual ranks of simmering beakers or curiously blinking contraptions. Rather, here is nothing more exotic than a "snowdrift of wasted paper" and strewn texts from shelves of arcane metaphysics. What ultimately emerges from that heap of "limp-leaved" texts is a tale of purely intellectual exploration, or what Tremaine had previously described as "thought variant." In this case, it seems Professor Mudge has stumbled upon a mathematical door to a "negative dimension," and has only to think of some distant location in order to physically transport himself. That he cannot control his thoughts, finally proves his undoing and so raises the recurring LRH theme involving failures to harness technological advancement.

Although indisputably astounding, this tale of a

John W. Campbell, Jr.

Arthur J. Burks

"The Dangerous Dimension,"
Astounding Science Fiction
magazine, July 1938.

teleporting professor was not, strictly speaking, science fiction. Ron himself would describe the work as fantasy, and essentially inspired from an Asian tradition of astral projection, i.e., that one's physical location may be altered by mere thought. Much more to the point of *Astounding,* was the second LRH offering, "The Tramp." Telling of a hobo endowed with extraordinary mental powers after experimental brain surgery, "The Tramp" is finally the tale of a Frankenstein's monster or experimentation gone awry. In that regard, the theme again involves a failure to harness technological advancement, and stood quite at odds with Campbell's equation of hard science as our sole salvation. With the advent of atomic weapons, however, more than a few from *Astounding* circles would join Ron at the Hollywood home of Robert Heinlein for discussions on ways of inspiring a peaceable space race instead of a nuclear arms race.

It is only with *Final Blackout,* however, that we come to the most fully realized LRH statement on this matter of a technological advance into oblivion. Initially appearing in April of 1940, and originally entitled "The Unkillables," the novel is consistently ranked among the ten greatest works of science fiction's golden age, rightfully compared to Orwell's *1984,* and certainly just as chilling. Yet again, *Final Blackout* is probably not science fiction as Campbell conceived it. Rather, the setting is a Europe just beyond Dunkirk—but a Europe so thoroughly battered, it finally resembles nothing less than a

moonscape. The central figure, known only as The Lieutenant, is arguably the most fully mythic character to ever emerge from the pages of *Astounding*:

"He was born in an air-raid shelter—and his first wail was drowned by the shriek of bombs, the thunder of falling walls and the coughing chatter of machine guns raking the sky.

"He was taught in a countryside where A was for Antiaircraft and Z was for Zeppelin. He knew that the improved Vickers Wellington bombers had flown clear to Moscow, but nobody thought to tell him about a man who had sailed a carrack twice as far in the opposite direction—a chap called Columbus.

"War-shattered officers had taught him the arts of battle on the relief maps of Rugby. Limping sergeants had made him expert with rifle and pistol, light and heavy artillery. And although he could not conjugate a single Latin verb, he was graduated as wholly educated at fourteen and commissioned the same year."

Once in the field, commands of the remains of an army were lost to "all causes and

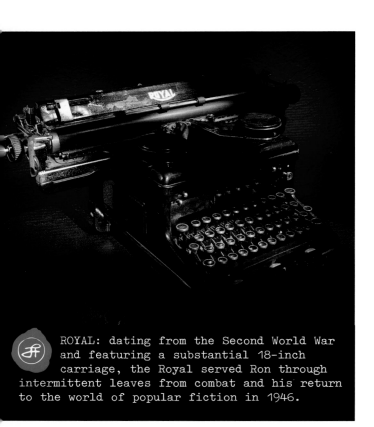

ROYAL: dating from the Second World War and featuring a substantial 18-inch carriage, the Royal served Ron through intermittent leaves from combat and his return to the world of popular fiction in 1946.

The Shaping of FEAR

*E*ventually, *those surrounding LRH would tell several apocryphal tales regarding his authorship of* Fear: *how the work had virtually possessed him, how it had first been conceived over barbecued steaks on John Campbell's New Jersey lawn, how Ron had furiously rewritten the work on a midnight train from Connecticut. None of it is verifiable, and the best description of how he came to author a tale of which so much would be said is found in his letters to friends from the third week in January 1940. Selections of these letters are reproduced here for the first time.*

Knickerbocker Hotel
January 18, 1940

. . . I have been so upset about a story for the past few days that I have not written to you, not wanting to even touch this mill. However I finally got the plot of it licked and am doing research upon it . . .

The story will be named PHANTASMAGORIA and the theme is, "What happened to Dwight Brown on the day he cannot remember?" Twenty-four hours lost from a man's life. And if I handle it properly it will be something Dostoevski might have done. He strives to locate his deeds while missing everywhere but in the right place, for he fears to look there. He is surrounded, day by day, by more terror and apparitions as his solutions are gathered about him only to become hollow and half seen. He knows, deep down, that the day he recognizes his deeds of the day he cannot remember, on that day he shall die. And, having gone mad he has to choose between being mad forever and being dead. And if you don't think that one was a tough one at which to arrive and now plot by incident . . . ! And John Campbell

> **"L. Ron Hubbard's *Fear* is one of the few books in the chiller genre which actually merits employment of the overworked adjective 'classic,' as in 'This is a classic tale of creeping, surreal menace and horror'... This is one of the really, really good ones."**
> **— Stephen King**

"Fear," Unknown magazine, July 1940 (left); Fear, hardcover, 1991 (center); and Fear, paperback, 1992 (right).

all the while drumming new suggestions at me and insisting I use them . . . ! And five conflicting stories to be woven into one . . . !!!!!!!

Knickerbocker Hotel
January 28, 1940

I tried, today, to start PHANTASMAGORIA, having fully outlined it last night. But for some reason I could not think connectedly enough or establish a sufficient mood. It is a pretty dolorous story and so I suppose I had better tell it very calmly and factually, without striving to dwell on mood. . . .

While I've been writing you some part of my head has been trying to coax up a certain tone for the story. And I think a nice, delicate style is best suited. Paint everything in sweetness and light and then begin to dampen it, not with the style, but with the events themselves. In other words lead the reader in all unsuspecting and then dump the works on his head. Show very little true sympathy and do not at all try to make the facts worse than they are but rather make light of them. Oh hell! This is such a hard story! But I can see a sleepy college town with spring and elms

> **"L. Ron Hubbard has been, since the 40's, one of the five writers in the SF field who have served me as models and teachers. His stories, *Fear* in particular, directly influenced all my work..."**
> **— Ray Faraday Nelson**

and yawning students and a man just back from an ethnological expedition, called to take over from a professor who has become ill. A man suited to quiet solitude with a certain still idealism about him, who has come back to his home and his wife and is trying anxiously to fit into the picture which he so long ago left. If told almost dispassionately the thing ought to be good. In other words, I'll just write it. For I can't work up a gruesome mood. Ah, for a few days out of my adolescence! The character must take it all mildly, that's the easiest way. How I hate to make anyone "emote"! . . .

"Final Blackout," Astounding Science Fiction, April 1940 (left); Final Blackout, hardcover, 1989, (center); and Final Blackout, paperback, 1992 (right).

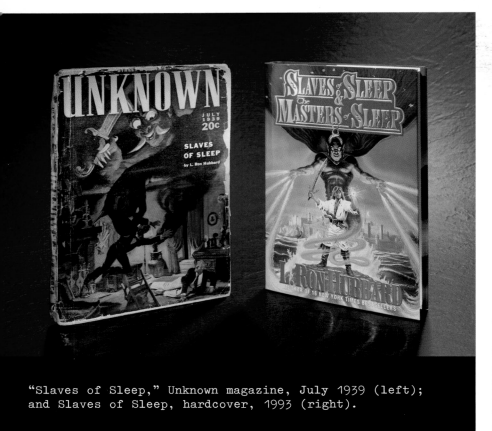

"Slaves of Sleep," Unknown magazine, July 1939 (left); and Slaves of Sleep, hardcover, 1993 (right).

"Final Blackout is as perfect a piece of science fiction as has ever been written."

— **Robert Heinlein**

"A landmark classic! It has been remembered through the decades as one of the all-time memorable classics of the science fiction field."

— **Robert Bloch**

* * *

connections," with faith in nothing beyond their lieutenant. Yet he was, "after all, a highly satisfactory god. He fed them, clothed them, and conserved their lives—which was more than any other god could have done." If the enemy is clearly fascist, the socialists are no ally. Nevertheless, the work is not a political statement; it is anti-war, and inevitably sparked no small controversy on that eve of international mobilization.

Concurrently, or nearly so, we find another sort of LRH work from the period, the adult fantasy. If the genre was tentatively approached by that teleporting Professor Mudge, it is first fully realized with "The Ultimate Adventure." Telling of a thoroughly modern trek into the realm of *A Thousand and One Nights*, the story was

* * *

"*Slaves of Sleep* became a sort of buzzword. There are bits and pieces from Ron's work that became part of the language in ways that very few other writers imagined."

— **Frederik Pohl**

"I particularly like *Typewriter in the Sky* because it was such a skillful parody of adventure fiction and was written with a great deal of lightness and touch which you didn't get much in those days."

— **James Gunn**
Science Fiction Historian, Professor of Literature

"An adventure story written in the great style adventure should be written in."
— **Clive Cussler**

* * *

the first of several to tap the world of Arabian myth and played no small part in Street & Smith's founding of *Unknown*—that most memorable of all fantasy vehicles, and expressly launched to accommodate the likes of the LRH tale.

On the heels of "The Ultimate Adventure," and also for the pages of *Unknown*, came the similarly inspired, "Slaves of Sleep." Again the setting is that never-never world of the *Arabian Nights*, and again the protagonist is thoroughly modern— in this case, a shipping magnate condemned to a simultaneous existence in parallel realms. Described as a prototypic tale of alternate dimensions, the work inspired much imitation; hence, the J. W. Campbell note to LRH: "I've been telling a few of the

* * *

"**Ole Doc Methuselah** resonates with the hum of high energy, captivating characters and great adventure...a cornucopia of fabulous adventure, wonderful characters and great fun."
— **Roddy McDowall**

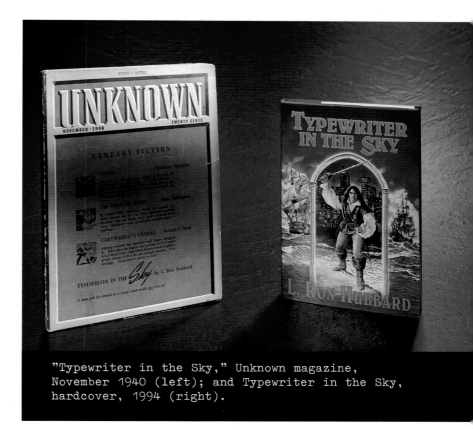

"Typewriter in the Sky," Unknown magazine, November 1940 (left); and Typewriter in the Sky, hardcover, 1994 (right).

One of seven Astounding Science Fiction issues containing installments of LRH's Ole Doc Methuselah novel (left); Ole Doc Methuselah, hardcover, 1992 (right).

> **"Science Fiction ... is the dream that precedes the dawn when the inventor or scientist awakens and goes to his books or his lab saying, 'I wonder whether I could make that dream come true in the world of real science.'"**
>
> **L. Ron Hubbard**

boys to read Washington Irving as an example of pure fantasy . . . and adding that they aren't to do *Arabian Nights* because the field is preempted by you." As of midsummer, 1940, however, LRH sights had already settled on still higher ground, and not easily followed.

As an introductory word, let us briefly consider a continuing topic of LRH interest extending from his ethnological work in the Caribbean and elsewhere— namely, the primitive's belief in unseen but "jealous beings anxious to undermine the happiness of man." The subject proved particularly fascinating owing to its universality; virtually all tribal communities subscribe to a cosmology of animistic demons. Of interest here, however, is what followed from that research in a purely literary sense—namely, the extraordinary tale of ethnologist James Lowry who must find four missing hours from his life. Originally entitled "Phantasmagoria," and rightly described as a

story of "metaphysical unease," it is a landmark work in every way and remembered today as *Fear*.

"If I handle it properly," reads an LRH note on the work in progress, "it will be something Dostoevski might have done." He was correct, and particularly when considering the hauntingly surreal *Notes from the Underground*. The work has also been compared to the best of Edgar Allan Poe, and just as legitimately so:

"Clouds, hard driven high up, occasionally flashed shadows over the pavement and lawns; the breeze close to earth frisked with the remnants of autumn, chasing leaves out of corners and across lawns against trees, bidding them vanish and make way for a new harvest later on."

But quite apart from all comparison, here is what literary historian David Hartwell described as among "the foundations of the contemporary modern horror genre," and work of profound "moral complexity that helped transform horror literature from antiquarian or metaphysical form into a contemporary and urban form with the gritty details of everyday realism." In that regard, he concludes, "From Ray Bradbury to Stephen King, a literary debt is owed to L. Ron Hubbard for *Fear*."

One could cite many more: *Fear* is probably the singly most celebrated work to have emerged from the whole of this pulp kingdom. One could also say much more: beyond *Fear*, stands a literal shelf of such fully unforgettable LRH works as "Typewriter in the Sky," "Ole Doc Methuselah," and that seminal tale of the time dilation theme, "To the Stars." But the time has now come to hear of these days from LRH himself.

Dating from 1969, and originally offered in response to requests from a commemorative review, comes the retrospective "By L. Ron Hubbard." To what Ron recounts in the way of incidental events from those golden years, let us understand that his pseudonymous Kurt von Rachen was to finally author several memorable tales for *Astounding* and *Unknown*, including such appropriately swashbuckling sf dramas as "The Idealist," "The Mutineers" and "The Rebels." Let us further understand that his mention of Willy Ley among Campbell, Asimov and Heinlein is especially meaningful; for if finally a minor author,

Despite the fact that only about 10 percent of his total body of fiction is composed of science fiction and fantasy L. Ron Hubbard helped to create what is still considered the great, classic "Golden Age of Science Fiction."

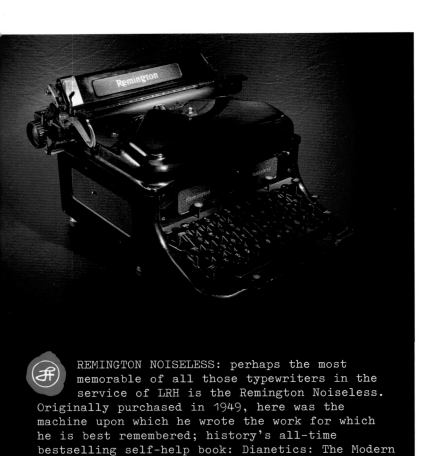

REMINGTON NOISELESS: perhaps the most memorable of all those typewriters in the service of LRH is the Remington Noiseless. Originally purchased in 1949, here was the machine upon which he wrote the work for which he is best remembered; history's all-time bestselling self-help book: Dianetics: The Modern Science of Mental Health.

"...to write, write and then write some more. And never to allow weariness, lack of time, noise, or any other thing to throw me off my course."

L. Ron Hubbard

Ley played no insignificant part in that popularization of the Space Age and is properly remembered as among the earliest proponents of rocket propulsion. Also significant is Ron's mention of Leo Margulies, then editorial director of *Thrilling Wonder Stories* and among the few to carry that pulp tradition into the 1950s.

In referencing "way stops" in Hollywood, Ron is speaking of his ten-week stint on the Columbia Pictures lot where he adapted his *Murder at Pirate Castle* to the screen as, *The Secret of Treasure Island*—a fifteen episode serial loosely inspired from adventures in the Caribbean and featuring murderous ghosts, an intrepid reporter and obligatory beauty. It was also through those typically productive ten weeks, Ron contributed to/doctored such big screen serials as *The Mysterious Pilot*, *The Adventures of Wild Bill Hickock* and (in conjunction with Norvell Page) *The Spider Returns*.

In citing the "petty squabbles," Ron is probably referencing the eventual feud between Campbell and A. J. Burks—apparently over money, and ultimately ending with the blackballing of Burks from the whole of science fiction. (If nothing else, recalled British author and editor George Hay, "Campbell was a man who knew how to hold a grudge.") In either case, Ron is perhaps too kind; the squabbles were not always petty, and he was finally the only author from the great pulp mainstream to survive Campbell's reign as science fiction czar.

By the same token, however, the friendship was real, and many an LRH letter tells of dinners at the Campbell home in the wastes of New Jersey, and lengthy lunches over plates of a "horrible ham" garnished with slices of pineapple. Campbell was additionally among the first to sense what Dianetics represented as the means by which we might venture into that greatest unknown of all, the universe of the self. Then, too, it was Campbell who, inspired by later LRH research, began calling for stories, not set in a distant future, but a prehistoric past—which, in turn, has arguably led to all we now celebrate as a new golden age of science fiction with tales from galaxies far away and a long, long time ago.

BY L. RON HUBBARD

HUBBARD

I guess I must have written the line "By L. Ron Hubbard" many thousands of times between 1930 and 1950.

And every time I wrote it I had a sense of starting something pleasing, something exciting and, it worked out, something that would sell. 93 1/2 percent of everything I wrote was accepted first draft, first submission.[1]

I wrote adventure, detective stories, air stories, science fiction, fantasy, technical articles, you name it.

Production was about 100,000 words a month most months, done on an electric typewriter, working an average of three hours a day, three days a week.

Arthur J. Burks, Ed Bodin, Bob Heinlein, John Campbell, Willy Ley, Isaac Asimov, these and the rest of the greats were my friends.

I shuttled between New York and Hollywood with way stops at a hideous rainy ranch in Puget Sound.

When I took time off, I went on expeditions to freshen up the old viewpoint.

I had one main problem, and that was running out of magazines to write for.

So I added about five pen names for stories to be "by."

One issue of one magazine was totally filled with my stories, once. All by different names.

It came about this way. Old-timers had editor problems. Editors were also readers. They got tired of one's stories but mainly got tired of the high prices they had to pay per word to a real pro.

So now and then an editor would cut you off his list for a while.

Once when this happened, I got even. I went back home and wrote a story, "The Squad That Never Came Back" and signed it "Kurt von Rachen." Then I had my agent, Ed Bodin, take it to dear old Leo Margulies (bless him) as something by a "new" writer.

Ed was scared stiff. "But if he finds out . . ."

I pushed him hard. It was a gag on Leo. So Ed did it.

Day or two later, Ed called me in a panic. "They love it. But they want to know what this guy looks like."

So I said, "He's a huge brute of a man. Tough. Black hair, beard. His idea of a party is to rent the floor of a hotel, get everybody drunk and smash the place to bits. A tough character."

So Ed hung up and all seemed well.

The next day he called again in even more of a panic, "They want to know where he is! They want to see him! And sign a contract!"

So I said, "He's in the Argentine. He's wanted for murder in Georgia!"

So Ed hung up. And all went through smoothly.

Now it's not illegal to use a pen name. But to play such a joke on an old friend like Leo was bad.

So I went over to Leo's office to tell him for laughs.

Unfortunately, Leo met me with a manuscript in his hand.

He said, "You old-time pros think you are all there is! Look at this. A story brand-new, fresh. New writer. Got it all over you."

And the manuscript he was holding was "The Squad That Never Came Back" by "Kurt von Rachen."

I let it go.

I used the name amongst others for some years. But that isn't all there is to the story.

After the war, years later, I was riding down in an elevator in Leo's building. A brand-new fresh writer had stepped in with me.

"I just sold three stories," he said.

I was glad for him. Most pros are for new young ones that are trying.

"Yeah," he said, "and this sure is a *wild* town," meaning New York.

"Last night I was at a party. Guy rented a whole floor of a hotel, got everybody drunk, smashed the place up . . ."

I started, blinked. Could it be?

"What was his name?" I inquired breathlessly.

"Kurt von Rachen," he said. And left me standing there forgetting to get out.

Oh, the old names, L. Sprague de Camp, Fletcher Pratt, Robert Bloch, Edmond Hamilton, Frank Belknap Long, dear old Edd Cartier and his fantastic beautiful illustrations, names still going, names forgotten.

We were quite a crew.

I look back now and love them all.

The petty squabbles, the friendly enmities.

All for the "By-line."

1. This figure is reflective of the LRH acceptance rate as of the late 1930s, or when he had established himself at the forefront of popular fiction.

A Final
Two Million
Words

HAVING DEVOTED THREE DECADES TO THE ADVANCEMENT OF DIANETICS
and Scientology beyond 1950, it was not until the 1980s we find L. Ron
Hubbard returning to the business of popular literature. In the interim,
the last of the pulps had quietly died, and the majority of those who had
filled the rough-cut pages had slipped into relative obscurity. (Although
what with eventual film adaptation the likes of "The Shadow," "The
Phantom," and "Doc Savage" would continue to dwell in popular
imagination.) One might further argue that much of what still endears us
to the pulps, including the stylized power of seasoned professionals with
several million words to their credit, was also lost. Hence, descriptions of
the modern novel as a "screenplay with the 'he said's' left in," i.e.,
narratively flat and prosaic. Hence, too, the quite unprecedented fervor
following word of L. Ron Hubbard's return to the field, and the actual
newspaper headlines: "Writer Resumes Career with Masterful Epic."

The Writing of Battlefield Earth

THAT EPIC—AND THE TERM IS FULLY ACCURATE—WAS *Battlefield Earth: A Saga of the Year 3000*. The work is nothing short of massive: "428,750 words long plus intro," as Ron finally calculated from the running tally with which he marked his daily progress. (Rather in awe, more than one critic would remark upon Ron's use of a then fairly rare word processor. In fact, however, he employed two Underwood manual typewriters—one to hammer out his several thousand words-a-day, while the other underwent repair. Every two or three weeks, he switched and proceeded to wear the alternate machine into a sorry state of disrepair.) Moreover, he was further to generate some seven hundred pages of handwritten notes, which further provide us some sense of how he approached the work.

The story, as meticulously detailed in those preliminary notes, tells of an earth so fully devastated after a thousand years of Psychlo rule, barely 35,000 human beings remain. Yet among those surviving humans is the wonderfully courageous Jonnie Goodboy Tyler. If he emerges from what is effectively a tribal community among the Rocky Mountains, he nonetheless proves more than a match for the inestimably cruel and technologically advanced Psychlos. Thus, the primary theme as reiterated in various ways through preliminary notes: the indomitable spirit of man prevailing over those who mistakenly regard him as an animal.

One finds the whole of the Psychlo history among those preliminary notes, including chronicles of interplanetary conquest, a discourse on galactic diplomacy and much concerning the tooth and claw mores of the rampaging Psychlos. The implication here: although John W. Campbell would speak of the LRH story as rolling out in a single creative burst, *Battlefield Earth* was plainly a work of very careful design and all the more impressive for the mere eight months of writing. Both setting and structure were firmly established before word one, while additional notes detailed technological advancements as extrapolated from a most impressive grasp of time-space theory. Also found among those initial notes is much of what provides the thematic continuity, with delineated chapter motifs and character sketches. Then, too, we find much pertaining to what is plainly satirical. Transcending even the power of the Psychlos is a race of intergalactic bankers (literal descendants of sharks) with a pressing lien on the entirety of earth, including existing resources, future proceeds from mineral exploitation, and even the destiny of future populations. If utterly unconcerned as to the fate of those on the balance sheets, the indifference is not malicious. Merely, "This is all just routine. Ordinary banking business."

The greater whole is precisely what critics declared: "an intergalactic adventure with the imagery and

The more than 700 pages of preliminary notes from the authorship of Battlefield Earth, which was written over an eight month period in 1980 and originally entitled, Man, the Endangered Species.

impact of *Star Wars* and a plot that sets it apart as a masterpiece." It was also rightly declared a blockbuster of phenomenal scope—riding one national bestseller list after another for a full year, then topping international lists—and a genuine *event* in publishing history. "It caught everyone by surprise when L. Ron Hubbard returned to writing," remarked an insider from the book trade, "the closest equivalent would have been the Dodgers coming home to Brooklyn." Then again, with initial sales of more than two million copies, one inevitably heard much talk of the book as a cultural catalyst in itself; *Battlefield Earth* has inspired an undying devotion among fans of the genre, and is regularly ranked among the six most memorable stories in the whole of science fiction along with Frank Herbert's *Dune* and Robert

Heinlein's *Stranger in a Strange Land.* The work has further become the basis of study in some forty institutions—appropriately including both George Washington and Harvard universities where LRH himself had lectured so many years earlier.

Finally, and of most immediate significance here, is all the novel came to represent as a legitimate trendsetter. The first work of science fiction in more than twenty years to attract a truly substantial mainstream readership (Heinlein's aforementioned *Stranger in a Strange Land* was the last), *Battlefield Earth* is legitimately credited with inspiring a resurgence for the whole of speculative fiction. Point of fact: within four years of *Battlefield Earth*'s publication, a once neglected speculative fiction—primarily fodder for the paperback original or specialty publisher—was suddenly accounting for a full 10 percent of all fiction sales. Hence the eventual descriptions of *Battlefield Earth* as "landmark," and "an epic which will be talked about for years to come."

The following LRH causerie has been hailed as a legitimate classic in its own right—specifically, "a delineating essay on science fiction as 'the herald of possibility' and fantasy as 'postulating no limits at all.' " To what has thus far been said of Ron's place in those wonderful realms of possibility, we might add one more pertinent word: in describing himself as initially diffident and, actually, "quite ignorant" of science fiction, Ron is touching upon yet another significant point of science fiction history. What originally fueled the field was not, as is so frequently argued, a John Campbell vision of brave new technological wonders penned by a stable of techno-authors from MIT and Cal Tech. No, what fueled science fiction was the same stuff fueling all great fiction—which is to say, all we have examined through "this business of writing."

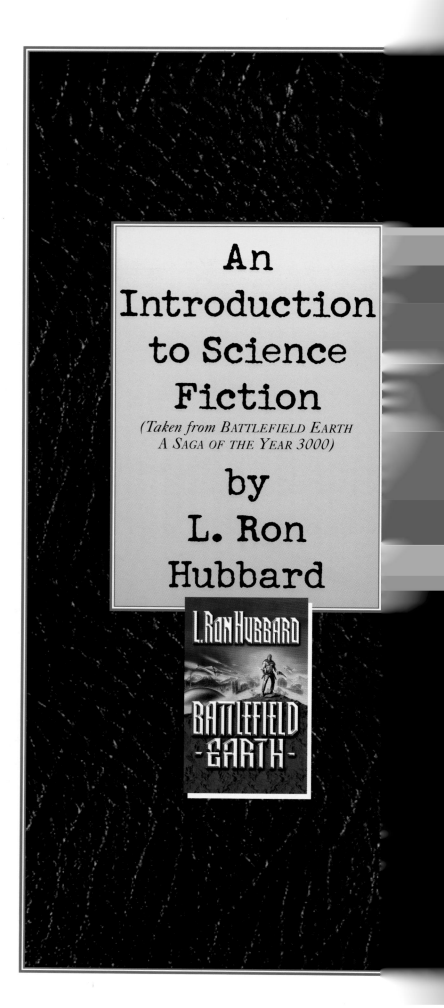

An Introduction to Science Fiction

(Taken from BATTLEFIELD EARTH A SAGA OF THE YEAR 3000)

by L. Ron Hubbard

Recently there came a period when I had little to do. This was novel in a life so crammed with busy years, and I decided to amuse myself by writing a novel that was <u>pure</u> science fiction.

In the hard-driven times between 1930 and 1950, I was a professional writer not simply because it was my job, but because I wanted to finance more serious researches. In those days there were few agencies pouring out large grants to independent workers. Despite what you might hear about Roosevelt "relief," those were depression years. One succeeded or one starved. One became a top-liner or a gutter bum. One had to work very hard at his craft or have no craft at all. It was a very challenging time for anyone who lived through it.

I have heard it said, as an intended slur, "He was a science fiction writer," and have heard it said of many. It brought me to realize that few people understand the role science fiction has played in the lives of Earth's whole population.

I have just read several standard books that attempt to define "science fiction" and to trace its history. There are many experts in this field, many controversial opinions. Science fiction is favored with the most closely knit reading public that may exist, possibly the most dedicated of any genre. Devotees are called "fans," and the word has a special prestigious meaning in science fiction.

Few professional writers, even those in science fiction, have written very much on the character

of "sf." They are usually too busy turning out the work itself to expound on what they have written. But there are many experts on this subject among both critics and fans, and they have a lot of worthwhile things to say.

However, many false impressions exist, both of the genre and of its writers. So when one states that he set out to write a work of <u>pure</u> science fiction, he had better state what definition he is using.

It will probably be best to return to the day in 1938 when I first entered this field, the day I met John W. Campbell, Jr., a day in the very dawn of what has come to be known as the golden age of science fiction. I was quite ignorant of the field and regarded it, in fact, a bit diffidently. I was not there of my own choice. I had been summoned to the vast old building on Seventh Avenue in dusty, dirty, old New York by the very top brass of Street & Smith publishing company--an executive named Black and another, F. Orlin Tremaine. Ordered there with me was another writer, Arthur J. Burks. In those days when the top brass of a publishing company--particularly one as old and prestigious as Street & Smith--"invited" a writer to visit, it was like being commanded to appear before the king or receiving a court summons. You arrived, you sat there obediently, and you spoke when you were spoken to.

We were both, Arthur J. Burks and I, top-line professionals in other writing fields. By the actual tabulation of A. B. Dick, which set advertising rates for publishing firms, either of our names appearing on a magazine cover would send the circulation rate skyrocketing, something like modern TV ratings.

The top brass came quickly to the point. They had recently started or acquired a magazine called Astounding Science Fiction. Other magazines were published by other houses, but Street & Smith was unhappy because its magazine was mainly publishing stories about machines and machinery. As publishers, its executives knew you had to have people in stories. They had called us in because, aside from our A. B. Dick rating as writers, we could write about real people. They knew we were busy and had other commitments. But would we be so kind as to write science fiction? We indicated we would.

They called in John W. Campbell, Jr., the editor of the magazine. He found himself looking at two adventure-story writers, and though adventure writers might be the aristocrats of the whole field and might have vast followings of their own, they were not science fiction writers. He resisted. In the first place, calling in top-liners would ruin his story budget due to their word rates. And in the second place, he had his own ideas of what science fiction was.

Campbell, who dominated the whole field of sf as its virtual czar until his death in 1971, was a huge man who had majored in physics at Massachusetts Institute of Technology and graduated from Duke University with a Bachelor of Science degree. His idea of getting a story was

Street & Smith was unhappy because its magazine was mainly publishing stories about machines and machinery.

to have some professor or scientist write it and then doctor it up and publish it. Perhaps that is a bit unkind, but it really was what he was doing. To fill his pages even he, who had considerable skill as a writer, was writing stories for the magazine.

The top brass had to directly order Campbell to buy and to publish what we wrote for him. He was going to get people into his stories and get something going besides machines.

I cannot tell you how many other writers were called in. I do not know. In all justice, it may have been Campbell himself who found them later on. But do not get the impression that Campbell was anything less than a master and a genius in his own right. Any of the stable of writers he collected during this golden age will tell you that. Campbell could listen. He could improve things. He could dream up little plot twists that were masterpieces. He well deserved the title that he gained and kept as the top editor and the dominant force that made science fiction as respectable as it became. Star Wars, the all-time box office record movie to date (exceeded only by its sequel), would never have happened if science fiction had not become as respectable as Campbell made it. More than that--Campbell played no small part in driving this society into the space age.

You had to actually work with Campbell to know where he was trying to go, what his idea was of this thing called "science fiction." I cannot give you any quotations from him; I can just tell you what I felt he was trying to do. In time we became friends. Over lunches and in his office and at his home on weekends--where his wife Doña kept things smooth--talk was always of stories but also of science. To say that Campbell considered science fiction as "prophecy" is an oversimplification. He had very exact ideas about it.

Only about a tenth of my stories were written for the fields of science fiction and fantasy. I was what they called a high-production writer, and these fields were just not big enough to take everything I could write. I gained my original reputation in other writing fields during the eight years before the Street & Smith interview.

Campbell, without saying too much about it, considered the bulk of the stories I gave him to be not science fiction but fantasy, an altogether different thing. Some of my stories he eagerly published as science fiction--among them Final Blackout. Many more, actually. I had, myself, somewhat of a science background, had done some pioneer work in rockets and liquid gases, but I was studying the branches of man's past knowledge at that time to see whether he had ever come up with anything valid. This, and a love of the ancient tales now called The Arabian Nights, led me to write quite a bit of fantasy. To handle this fantasy material, Campbell introduced another magazine, Unknown. As long as I was writing novels for it, it continued. But the war came and I and others went, and I think Unknown only lasted about forty months. Such

> Only about a tenth of my stories were written for the fields of science fiction and fantasy.... I gained my original reputation in other writing fields...

novels were a bit hard to come by. And they were not really Campbell's strength.

So anyone seeking to say that science fiction is a branch of fantasy or an extension of it is unfortunately colliding with a time-honored professional usage of terms. This is an age of mixed genres. I hear different forms of music mixed together like soup. I see so many different styles of dance tangled together into one "dance" that I wonder whether the choreographers really know the different genres of dance anymore. There is abroad today the concept that only conflict produces new things. Perhaps the philosopher Hegel introduced that, but he also said that war was necessary for the mental health of the people and a lot of other nonsense. If all new ideas have to spring from the conflict between old ones, one must deny that virgin ideas can be conceived.

So what would pure science fiction be?

It has been surmised that science fiction must come from an age where science exists. At the risk of raising dispute and outcry--which I have risked all my life and received but not been bothered by, and have gone on and done my job anyway--I wish to point out some things:

Science fiction does not come after the fact of a scientific discovery or development. It is the herald of possibility. It is the plea that someone should work on the future. Yet it is not prophecy. It is the dream that precedes the dawn when the inventor or scientist awakens and goes to his books or his lab saying, "I wonder whether I could make that dream come true in the world of real science."

You can go back to Lucian, second century A.D., or to Johannes Kepler (1571-1630)--who founded modern dynamical astronomy and who also wrote Somnium, an imaginary space flight to the moon--or to Mary Shelley and her Frankenstein, or to Poe or Verne or Wells and ponder whether this was really science fiction. Let us take an example: a man invents an eggbeater. A writer later writes a story about an eggbeater. He has not, thereby, written science fiction. Let us continue the example: a man writes a story about some metal that, when twiddled, beats an egg, but no such tool has ever before existed in fact. He has now written science fiction. Somebody else, a week or a hundred years later, reads the story and says, "Well, well. Maybe it could be done." And makes an eggbeater. But whether or not it was possible that twiddling two pieces of metal would beat eggs, or whether or not anybody ever did it afterward, the man still has written science fiction.

> Science fiction does not come after the fact of a scientific discovery or development. It is the herald of possibility. It is the plea that someone should work on the future.

How do you look at this word "fiction"? It is a sort of homograph. In this case it means two different things. A professor of literature knows it means "a literary work whose content is produced by the imagination and is not necessarily based on fact; the category of literature comprising works of this kind, including novels, short stories, and plays." It is

derived from the Latin fictio, a making, a fashioning, from fictus, past participle of fingere, to touch, form, mold.

But when we join the word to "science" and get "science fiction," the word "fiction" acquires two meanings in the same use: 1) the science used in the story is at least partly fictional; and 2) any story is fiction. The American Heritage Dictionary of the English Language defines science fiction as "fiction in which scientific developments and discoveries form an element of plot or background; especially a work of fiction based on prediction of future scientific possibilities."

So, by dictionary definition and a lot of discussions with Campbell and fellow writers of that time, science fiction has to do with the material universe and sciences; these can include economics, sociology, medicine, and suchlike, all of which have a material base.

Then what is fantasy?

Well, believe me, if it were simply the application of vivid imagination, then a lot of economists and government people and such would be fully qualified authors! Applying the word "imaginative" to fantasy would be like calling an entire library "some words." Too simplistic, too general a term.

In these modern times many of the ingredients that make up "fantasy" as a type of fiction have vanished from the stage. You hardly even find them in encyclopedias anymore. These subjects were spiritualism, mythology, magic, divination, the supernatural, and many other fields of that type. None of them had anything really to do with the real universe. This does not necessarily mean that they never had any validity or that they will not again arise; it merely means that man, currently, has sunk into a materialistic binge.

The bulk of these subjects consists of false data, but there probably never will come a time when <u>all</u> such phenomena are explained. The primary reason such a vast body of knowledge dropped from view is that material science has been undergoing a long series of successes. But I do notice that every time modern science thinks it is down to the nitty-gritty of it all, it runs into (and sometimes adopts) such things as the Egyptian myths that man came from mud, or something like that. But the only point I am trying to make here is that there is a whole body of phenomena that we cannot classify as "material." They are the nonmaterial, nonuniverse subjects. And no matter how false many of the old ideas were, they still existed; who knows but what there might not be some validity in some bits of them. One would have to study these subjects to have a complete comprehension of all the knowledge and beliefs possible. I am not opening the door to someone's saying I believe in all these things: I am only saying that there is another realm besides dedicated--and even simple-minded--materialism.

"Fantasy," so far as literature is concerned, is

Then what is fantasy?

Well, believe me, if it were simply the application of vivid imagination, then a lot of economists and government people and such would be fully qualified authors!

defined in the dictionary as "literary or dramatic fiction characterized by highly fanciful or supernatural elements." Even that is a bit limited as a definition.

So fantasy could be called any fiction that takes up elements such as spiritualism, mythology, magic, divination, the supernatural, and so on. <u>The Arabian Nights</u> was a gathering together of the tales of many, many countries and civilizations--not just of Arabia as many believe. Its actual title was <u>A Thousand and One Nights of Entertainment</u>. It abounds with examples of fantasy fiction.

When you mix science fiction with fantasy you do not have a pure genre. The two are, to a professional, separate genres. I notice today there is a tendency to mingle them and then excuse the result by calling it "imaginative fiction." Actually they don't mix well: science fiction, to be credible, has to be based on some degree of plausibility; fantasy gives you no limits at all. Writing science fiction demands care on the part of the author; writing fantasy is as easy as strolling in the park. (In fantasy, a guy has no sword in his hand; bang, there's a magic sword in his hand.) This doesn't say one is better than the other. They are simply very different genres from a professional viewpoint.

But there is more to this: science fiction, particularly in its golden age, had a mission. I cannot, of course, speak for my friends of that period. But from Campbell and from "shooting the breeze" with other writers of the time, one got the very solid impression that they were doing a heavy job of beating the drum to get man to the stars.

At the beginning of that time, science fiction was regarded as a sort of awful stepchild in the world of literature. But worse than that, science itself was not getting the attention or the grants or the government expenditures it should have received. There has to be a <u>lot</u> of public interest and demand before politicians shell out the financing necessary to get a subject whizzing.

Campbell's crew of writers were pretty stellar. They included very top-liner names. They improved the literary quality of the genre. And they began the boom of its broader popularity.

A year or so after the golden age began, I recall going into a major university's science department. I wanted some data on cytology for my own serious researches. I was given a courteous reception and was being given the references when I noticed that the room had been gradually filling up. And not with students but with professors and deans. It had been whispered around the offices who was in the biology department, and the next thing I knew, I was shaking a lot of hands held out below beaming faces. And what did they want to know: What did I think of this story or that? And had I seen this or that writer lately? And how was Campbell?

<u>They</u> had a literature! <u>Science</u> <u>fiction</u>!

And they were proud of it!

For a while, before and after World War II, I was in rather steady association with the new era of scientists, the boys who built the bomb, who

...science fiction, to be credible, has to be based on some degree of plausibility; fantasy gives you no limits at all.

were beginning to get the feel of rockets. They were all science fiction buffs. And many of the hottest scientists around were also writing science fiction on the side.

In 1945 I attended a meeting of old scientist and science fiction friends. The meeting was at the home of my dear friend, the incomparable Bob Heinlein. And do you know what was their agenda? How to get man into space fast enough so that he would be distracted from further wars on Earth. And they were the lads who had the government ear and authority to do it! We are coming close to doing it. The scientists got man into space and they even had the Russians cooperating for a while.

One can't go on living a naive life believing that everything happens by accident, that events simply follow events, that there is a natural order of things and that everything will come out right somehow. That isn't science. That's fate, kismet, and we're back in the world of fantasy. No, things do get planned. The golden age of science fiction that began with Campbell and <u>Astounding</u> <u>Science</u> <u>Fiction</u> gathered enough public interest and readership to help push man into space. Today, you hear top scientists talking the way we used to talk in bull sessions so long ago.

Campbell did what he set out to do. So long as he had his first wife and others around him to remind him that science was for <u>people</u>, that it was no use to just send machines out for the sake of machines, that there was no point in going into space unless the mission had something to do with people, too, he kept winning. For he was a very brilliant man and a great and very patient editor. After he lost his first wife, Doña, in

1949--she married George O. Smith--and after he no longer had a sounding board who made him keep people in stories, and when he no longer had his old original writing crew around, he let his magazine slip back, and when it finally became named Analog, his reign was over. But the golden age had kicked it all into high gear. So Campbell won after all.

When I started out to write this novel, I wanted to write pure science fiction. And not in the old tradition. Writing forms and styles have changed, so I had to bring myself up to date and modernize the styles and patterns. To show that science fiction is not science fiction because of a particular kind of plot, this novel contains practically every type of story there is --detective, spy, adventure, western, love, air-war, you name it. All except fantasy; there is none of that. The term "science" also includes economics and sociology and medicine where these are related to material things. So they're in here, too.

In writing for magazines, the editors (because of magazine format) force one to write to exact lengths. I was always able to do that-- it is a kind of knack. But this time I decided not to cut everything out and to just roll her as she rolled, so long as the pace kept up. So I may have wound up writing the biggest sf novel ever in terms of length. The experts--and there are lots of them to do so--can verify whether this is so.

Some of my readers may wonder that I did not include my own serious subjects in this book. It was with no thought of dismissal of them. It was just that I put on my professional writer's hat. I also did not want to give anybody the idea I was doing a press relations job for my other serious works.

The golden age of science fiction that began with Campbell and Astounding Science Fiction gathered enough public interest and readership to help push man into space.

There are those who will look at this book and say, "See? We told you he is just a science fiction writer!" Well, as one of the crew of writers that helped start man to the stars, I'm very proud of also being known as a science fiction writer. You have satellites out there, man has walked on the moon, you have probes going to the planets, don't you? Somebody had to dream the dream, and a lot of somebodies like those great writers of the golden age and later had to get an awful lot of people interested in it to make it true.

I hope you enjoy this novel. It is the only one I ever wrote just to amuse myself. It also celebrates my golden wedding with the muse. Fifty years a professional-- 1930-1980.

And as an old pro I assure you that it is pure science fiction. No fantasy. Right on the rails of the genre. Science is for people. And so is science fiction.

Ready?

Stand by.

Blast off!

L. Ron Hubbard October 1980

"[*Battlefield Earth*] has everything: suspense, pathos, politics, war, humor, diplomacy and intergalactic finance... Hubbard keeps things moving so irresistibly... and the 800 pages go by quickly."

- Publishers Weekly

* * *

"Good old fashioned space opera (Buck Rogers stuff) makes a solid comeback in L. Ron Hubbard's *Battlefield Earth*... If you think they don't write 'em anymore like they used to, take heart -- here's 800 pages from one of the originals."

- New York Newsday

* * *

"Think of the *Star Wars* sagas, and *Raiders of the Lost Ark*, mix in the triumph of *Rocky I*, *Rocky II* and *Rocky III* and you have captured the exuberance, style and glory of *Battlefield Earth*."

-Baltimore Evening Sun

* * *

"Without a doubt, L. Ron Hubbard is one of the most prolific and influential writers of the twentieth century."

- Stephen V. Whaley, PhD
Professor of English and
Foreign Languages

Battlefield Earth, the perennial international bestseller. Thus far, it has been translated into 13 languages and released in more than 15 countries. It is without a doubt the most popular single-volume science fiction novel of the last two decades.

Satire is
healthy stuff.
It gets people to
laugh at things
they have been
in awe or horror of.

Laughter is the
earliest therapy
When you can do
nothing else you
can always laugh.

In addition to the 1.2 million word Mission Earth manuscript, LRH compiled more than 1,500 pages of handwritten notes wherein he sketched every chapter, every character and a wealth of relevant technical information.

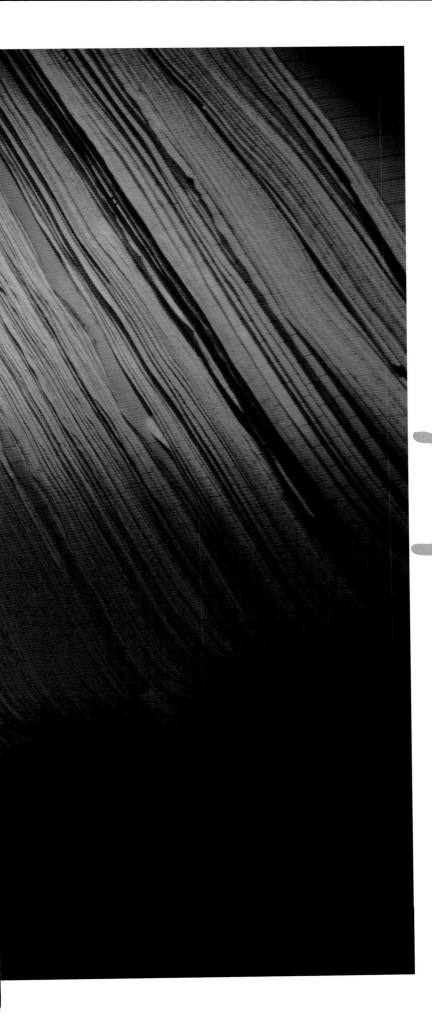

The Magnum Opus: Mission Earth

BATTLEFIELD EARTH WAS NOT, HOWEVER—AS MANY a critic initially declared—the LRH *magnum opus*. Rather, that distinction is more generally afforded to the next of the final LRH works, the ten volume, 1.2 million word, *Mission Earth* series. How he managed those 1.2 million words in what amounted to the space of twelve months is yet another of those legendary literary feats in line with the perfect dictated sentences of the later Henry James or the virtually flawless hand-written manuscripts of the later Charles Dickens. In either case, the LRH rate of production alone is astonishing, actually surpassing his fabled speed in the heyday of pulps, and even more impressive considering those rotating Underwood manuals—one in the shop for repair, while he rapidly wore down the other and then switched.

"SF and fantasy hold out the prospect of possibility and in possibility you have choice and in choice you have freedom and <u>there</u> you have touched on the basic nature of every person."

- L. Ron Hubbard

Again, a mass of preliminary notes reveals an intricate plan behind all that seems so freely wrought—every chapter carefully outlined, every character neatly sketched. The whole is a wonderfully wrought tale of a suave and swashbuckling Fleet Combat Engineer from the planet Voltar who must battle a nefarious intelligence chief to save an unsuspecting earth and thwart the subversion of Voltar itself. The whole represents an after-the-fact confession from former Coordinated Information Apparatus (CIA) executive Soltan Gris, and otherwise employs a uniquely villainous viewpoint; the intrepid combat engineer, Jettero Heller, has been implanted with a video-relayer allowing Gris to see and hear all our hero experiences. What ensues is a perfectly wry and ironic assessment of a well-intentioned and capable hero— as when this Soltan Gris insists we view Heller as a hopeless innocent among savagely clever CIA operatives . . . even as Heller effortlessly outwits them all.

"I loved *Mission Earth*" declared Ray Faraday Nelson of the genre's new wave, "The CIA will hate it." He was undoubtedly correct, and particularly in light of later charges that Agency personnel had been financing Central American operations with profits from the heroin trade—all as more or less portrayed in the pages of *Mission Earth*. Similarly, there is all *Mission Earth* has to say concerning drug enforcement officials on the take—more or less in line with later scandals involving Mexican enforcement agencies—and all else the earth-raping multinationals, death-dealing bureaucracies, conniving media, casual murder and rampant immorality. Or as yet another critic described it, "in a biting commentary on exactly who is doing what on today's earth."

The statement is supremely apt, and actually even more so given what the shape of society as we approach the new millennium. For example, much of Heller's trials involve his efforts to salvage earth from wanton pollution at the hands of a John Delbert Rockecenter and the Seven Brothers, i.e., the Seven Sisters.[1] In the process, Heller stumbles upon an alien plot to subvert Voltarian society with several thousand tons of Turkish opium. (Although physiologically superior in certain respects, Voltarians are nonetheless subject to the same dark temptations as the earthling.) The result: an utterly pandemic drug abuse crisis, much like what we suffer today. There is likewise much regarding the patently illegal methods of law enforcement agencies, (as in a Federal Bureau of Investigation now known to have wiretapped the telephones of United States congressional representatives), and the employment of a J. Walter Madison to keep the reading public fully uninformed—as in the J. Walter Thompson public relations conglomerate representing highly dubious medical, pharmaceutical and petroleum interests, and lately charged with helping to incite the Gulf War. Finally, there is also much on the psychiatric and psychological encouragement of sexual perversion as a means of population control—all under a banner

1. Seven Sisters: Exxon, Mobil, Chevron, Texaco, Gulf, Royal Dutch Shell and British Petroleum.

Rather in awe of the 430,000 word Battlefield Earth, more than one critic would remark upon Ron's use of a then fairly rare word processor. In fact, however, he employed these two conveniently portable Underwood manual typewriters -- one to hammer out his several thousand words-a-day, while the other underwent repair. Although the bottom of the Underwood line, these plastic-cased manuals proved the only machine capable of accommodating Ron's legendary typing speed in writing both Mission Earth and Battlefield Earth.

of "Mental Stealth" and all perfectly in line with the smorgasbord of sexual perversion now advertised everywhere under that ever-popular euphemism, "The Alternative Lifestyle."

The point—and this from a secretary/research assistant charged with collecting the small mountain of background literature—*Mission Earth* is a work of definitive satire and expressly intended "for the raising of social consciousness." If the world portrayed is the height of hypocrisy—where the most saintly are, in fact, the most outlandishly criminal, where political and corporate corruption is the order of the day and populations are regarded as sheep for the slaughter—nothing is accidental, nothing just a byproduct of human genetics as psychiatry would have us believe. Rather, there are explicit reasons for all that plagues this planet, and those reasons are both identifiable and

L. RON HUBBARD
AUTHOR OF THE GIANT BESTSELLER "BATTLEFIELD EARTH"

MISSION EARTH VOLUME 1

THE INVADERS PLAN

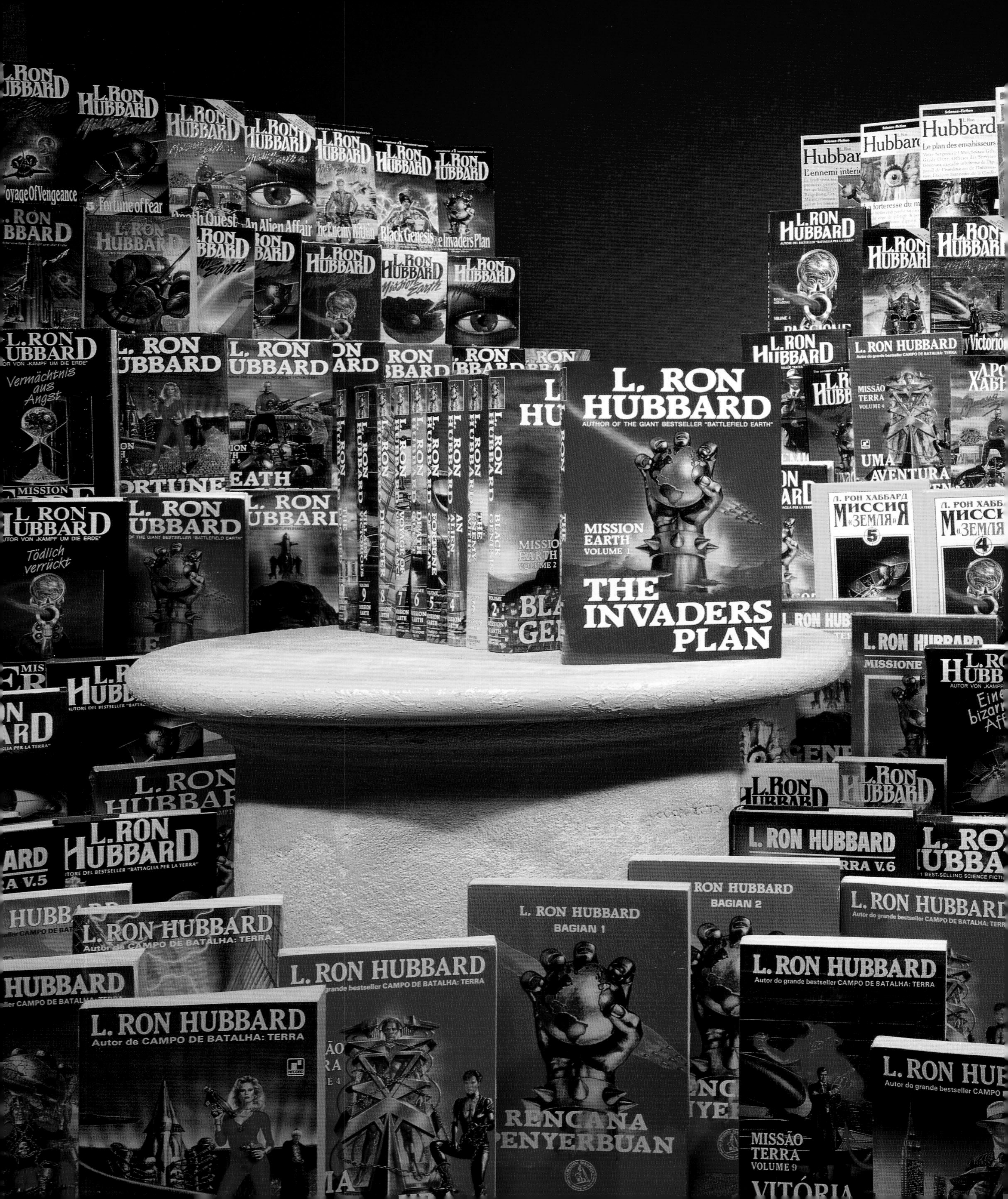

"I loved *Mission Earth*. The CIA will hate it. Hubbard has produced a real knee-slapper... he's laughing at the sacred cow of the eighties, the so-called intelligence community... Few writers have had the knack of making a serious philosophical point without ever stopping to preach, without ever slowing the action for an instant."

—Ray Faraday Nelson

* * *

"We do not collect trendy authors, nor do we collect minor authors. In the field of American literature, for instance, we select with care only those American or Californian authors who we determine are important contributors to the state, to the country and to the world. L. Ron Hubbard is perhaps <u>the</u> quintessential western author, and his works fit perfectly in our collection."

—Thomas V. Lange
The Huntington Library

* * *

"*The Invaders Plan* [Volume 1, *Mission Earth*] reads like an intergalactic *Raiders of the Lost Ark*. Once you start you'll be hard pressed to put the book down. On our scale of 1 to 10 with 10 being excellent, *The Invaders Plan* comes out at 10. It's fabulous and fun reading.

—United Press International

resolvable. It's simply a question of cutting through that J. Walter Madison double talk and the psychobabble from a world association of "Mental Stealth," and getting to the source of the problem. Although as Jettero Heller so painfully discovers, "the way this planet is organized, apparently, is that if you try to do anything to help it, some special interest group jumps all over you." As something of a footnote here, it might further be mentioned that much of what the series satirically addresses, LRH himself very seriously addressed as both the Founder of Scientology, and founder of the world's most singularly effective programs for drug rehabilitation, criminal reform and moral regeneration. In other words, as a genuine opponent of those forces which underlie criminality, drug abuse and immorality, here is an author who knows of what he writes.

What such insight ultimately made for is a work of truly phenomenal and enduring popularity. As noted, each consecutive volume of the *Mission Earth* dekalogy successively rose to international bestseller lists until those lists were all but filled with *Mission Earth*. At one point, readers found no less than seven *Mission Earth* volumes among the ten bestselling hardcover books, prompting author and professor of journalism James Gunn to declare, "I don't know anything in publishing history to compare with it." As further noted, the series is now routinely described as a legitimate classic, repeatedly drawing comparison to the works of Jonathan Swift, and so prompting golden age author/editor Damon Knight to summarize the LRH impact as absolutely unequivocal: "He cut a swath across the science-fiction fantasy world the likes of which has never been seen." Finally there is all *Mission Earth* has come to represent "as a milestone work of mainstream fiction," to cite yet another critic, and all else the series represents in terms of what its author described as "a plea that someone should work on the future."

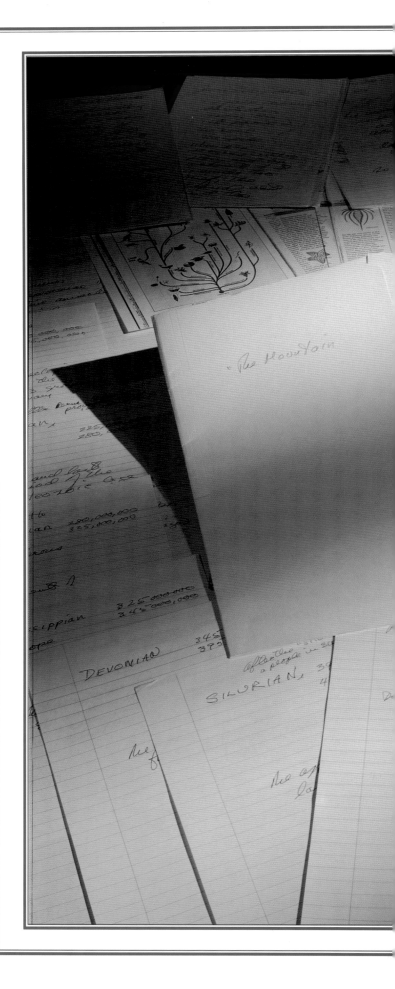

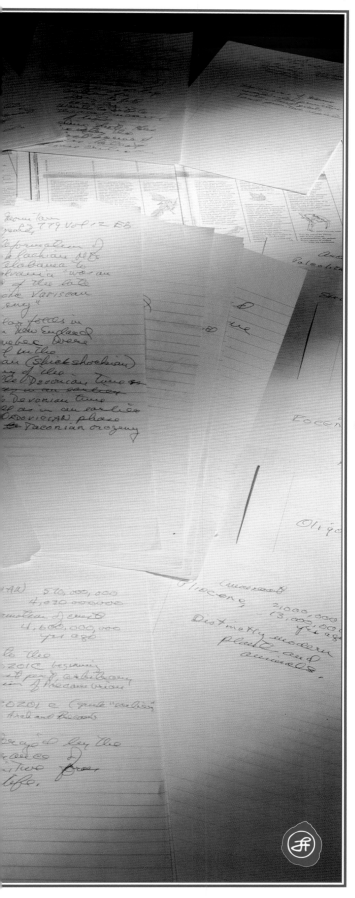

The Unfinished Mountain

Among the larger body of LRH manuscripts, are the few but fascinating pages from an unfinished novel entitled, "The Mountain." That many an author leaves an incomplete manuscript or unrealized outline is typical; for true authorship is generally a lifelong pursuit and not a career from which one retires. Consequently, we come upon the notes and first pages of the LRH work-in-progress as of his passing in 1986.

A charming fable for all ages, the story tells of a cruel and materialist mountain anxious to recount his considerable history before the onslaught of bulldozers and the laying of pavement. That history is, in turn, passed to a sleeping author—"worn with ink-stained fingers"—through the medium of dream. Thus unfolds a four-billion-year tale of geological and biological development. "He's always thought that he himself was God," reads an LRH note on the character of that mountain, but finally comes to "suspect there might be some other God that has just been using him." There is also much on the emergence of increasingly complex cellular life forms—a deeply resented encroachment in the mountain's materialist view—and a final affirmation of things spiritual which runs through the finest LRH.

L. RON HUBBARD'S

WRITERS OF THE FUTURE

Given the traditionally difficult path from first manuscript to published novel—and particularly so in an era when publishers tend to devote the lion's share of advertising budgets to but a few household names—L. Ron Hubbard "initiated a means for new and budding writers to have a chance for their creative efforts to be seen and acknowledged." That means was his Writers of The Future Contest. Established in 1983, expressly for the unpublished novelist (candidates may have previously published three short stories or a novelette), Writers of The Future has subsequently become the most respected and significant forum for new talent in the whole of the fantasy and science fiction realm. Accordingly, judges are drawn from among the most celebrated names of the genre, including: Robert Silverberg, Frank Herbert, Jerry Pournelle, Andre Norton, Anne McCaffrey

THE L. RON HUBBARD GOLD AWARD (BELOW LEFT),
PRESENTED ANNUALLY TO THE WINNER OF THE
WRITERS OF THE FUTURE CONTEST.
FINALISTS AND WINNERS OF THE L. RON HUBBARD
WRITERS OF THE FUTURE CONTEST
ARE PUBLISHED IN ANNUAL ANTHOLOGIES.
FOR MANY WINNERS THIS PROVIDES THE CATALYST
FOR A PROFESSIONAL WRITING CAREER.

The first L. Ron Hubbard Gold Award presented by Jack Williamson and Anne McCaffrey at the 1984 awards ceremony in Beverly Hills.

L. Ron Hubbard Achievement Awards presented to the winners of the 1994 (center) and 1995 (bottom, left) Writers of The Future Contest. Ceremonies at Houston's Space Center included writing workshop sessions and symposium on "Man's Role in Space" (top left) with panelist Astronaut Dr. Story Musgrave (bottom, right).

Winner in 1993 (left) and finalist in 1991 (below) are presented their awards.

and—longtime LRH friends from that fabled golden age—Jack Williamson and C. L. Moore.

In addition to cash awards, winning entries are annually published in *L. Ron Hubbard Presents Writers of The Future* anthology—the bestselling new fiction anthology of its kind, and a proven springboard for the future publication of contributors. Point of fact: since inception, the contest has helped place more than a hundred new novels on American shelves, has launched the professional careers of 150 young authors, and has otherwise rightfully earned the description "a credit to American literature and a singular, generous event." The Writers of The Future has further rightfully earned a place alongside the Hugo and Nebula awards as the third in a triad of the genre's primary acknowledgments for literary excellence.

In recognition of what that award now represents to both those who author speculative literature and those whom it most inspires, the Writers of The Future awards ceremony enjoys participation from among the world's most celebrated scientific figures on the most distinguished forums. Nobel winning physicist Dr. Sheldon Glashow, for example, served as panelist for award ceremonies at the United Nations, while astronaut Story Musgrave (of Hubble repair fame and "the oldest man in space") served in the same capacity for ceremonies

Writers of The Future winners at the 11th annual awards ceremony. After winning the L. Ron Hubbard Writers of The Future Contest, winners have gone on to sell nearly 100 novels and 1,000 short stories.

at National Aeronautics and Space Administration's Space Center in Houston, Texas.

The Writers of The Future awards ceremony was additionally the first such symposium within the United Nation's Trusteeship Council Chamber, and thus the first presentation of speculative fiction on a truly international stage. Hosting the event, one should further note, was none other than Hans W. Janitschek, President of the United Nation's Society of Writers, who appropriately cited all L. Ron Hubbard has come to represent as an inspiration for millions, "and awakening the genius of writing in thousands."

Also springing from Writers of The Future is the L. Ron Hubbard Writing Workshop, initially held in 1985 and affording contest winners personal critique and instruction by such undisputed masters of the craft as editor/author Algis Budrys and the previously discussed Frederik Pohl. Similarly styled L. Ron Hubbard Writing Workshops have been instituted at Harvard, Duke and Brigham Young universities where students are invited to examine much of what is found in the LRH instructional essays reprinted here.

The 1989 L. Ron Hubbard Awards at the United Nations where awards were presented (left) in the Trusteeship Council Chamber (bottom). Writers of The Future symposium, at the World Trade Center addressed by Isaac Asimov (center).

Library of Congress.

George Washington University.

United States National Archives.

The L. Ron Hubbard's Writing Workshops where young authors are privileged with instruction from the masters, and Ron's own 50 years in the trade.

Writers of The Future Contest judges have included (above, left to right) Kelly Freas, Ramsey Campbell, Larry Niven and Frederik Pohl.

The international acclaim for his literary achievements and contributions to the field of the arts is evident in the countless recognitions and awards bestowed upon L. Ron Hubbard. Shown here is but a sampling of the types of awards which continue to be received on L. Ron Hubbard's behalf by his literary representatives and publishers in the United States and abroad.

A Closing Note

In 1986, to meet a continuing demand for the works of L. Ron Hubbard, the LRH literary agency of Author Services, Inc. commenced a twenty-year schedule for the republication of all early LRH fiction and all remaining unpublished works. *Fear* and *Final Blackout,* among the first of those works to see reprint, promptly leapt to bestseller lists in a telling restatement of popularity from fifty years earlier. Among other titles slated for publication are two comedic LRH screenplays, *Ai! Pedrito!* and *A Very Strange Trip,* Ron authorized for novelization by those following in his footsteps through his Writers of The Future program among other authors. (More will be said on these screenplays in *Ron: The Filmmaker.*) Also slated for reprint is much of what originally endeared Ron to readers of *Argosy* and *Five Novels Monthly,* more again from the pages of *Thrilling Adventures* and *Detective Fiction Weekly,* still more from the likes of *Astounding* and *Unknown* . . . until, at last, readers may conveniently examine the whole of the L. Ron Hubbard literary legacy, some four hundred titles in all.

What that legacy finally represents is, of course, what has been variously stated by authors and critics through the pages of this publication: here is a writer who stands among the most influential and widely read authors of all time, with an astonishing 114 million published copies of fiction and nonfiction in more than a hundred nations and thirty languages. Here is a "creator of the first order, blessed with an imagination beyond description," as Hans Janitschek so eloquently phrased it. Or even more simply, here is an author who has shown us what this business of writing is finally all about.

My salvation
is to let all this
roll over me, to write,
write and write
some more.
To hammer keys until
I am finger worn
to the second joint
and then to hammer
keys some more.
To pile up copy,
stack up stories,
roll the wordage and
generally conduct
my life along
the one line of success
I have ever had.
I write."

L. Ron Hubbard